The

MENTALLY TOUGH ONLINE TRADER

A Sanity Guide for the Totally Wired Investor

ROBERT KOPPEL

DEARBORN™
A **Kaplan Professional** Company

Associate Publisher: Cynthia A. Zigmund
Senior Managing Editor: Jack Kiburz
Senior Project Editor: Trey Thoelcke
Interior Design: Lucy Jenkins
Cover Design: Scott Rattray, Rattray Design
Typesetting: the dotted i

© 2000 by Robert Koppel

Published by Dearborn, a Kaplan Professional Company

Printed in the United States of America

00 01 02 10 9 8 7 6 5 4 3 2 1

Library of Congress Cataloging-in-Publication Data

Koppel, Robert.
        The mentally tough online trader / Robert Koppel.
        p.   cm.
        Includes index.
        ISBN 0-7931-3809-4
        1. Electronic trading of securities—Psychological aspects.   2. Investments—Psychological aspects.   3. Investment analysis—Psychological aspects.
        I. Title.
        HG4515.95.K66 2000
        332.64′2′0285—dc21   00-029464

TO MY FAMILY

Mara, Lily, and Niko

To perform toward the upper limit of our physical skill and
talent brings us face to face with ourselves; our insecurities,
doubts, inadequacies and fears . . . mastery is a contest
of each person against oneself.

—*James E. Loehr*, Mental Toughness Training for Sports

You've got to be careful if you don't know where you are
going because you might not get there.

—*Yogi Berra*

Contents

Foreword   vii
Preface   xi
Acknowledgments   xv

P A R T 1 Investing Online

1. Investing Online   3
2. What Kind of Investor Are You?   19

P A R T 2 The Psychological Skills of the Online Trader

3. Motivation   35
4. Setting Goals   43
5. Developing Confidence   67
6. Controlling Anxiety   81
7. Focusing and Managing Your State of Mind   91
8. Using Positive Imagery   103

P A R T 3 Technical Analysis for the Online Trader

9. The Psychology of Technical Analysis   113
10. Chart Analysis and Trends   125
11. More about Trends   133
12. Active Online Trading   147
13. Technical Considerations for Swing Trading   159
14. Moving from One Winning Stock Trade to Another   189

P A R T 4 The Successful Online Trader

15. Becoming a Mentally Tough Trader: Competing on a
    Level Playing Field   205

For Further Reading   219
Glossary   221
Index   227
About the Author   235

Foreword

OK, I admit it. I'm an active online trader. Attracted initially by the almost illicit pleasures of being a quick reacting "SOES bandit," I honed a rapid-fire scalping ability that generated regular profits. Then, with surprising suddenness, market conditions changed and those easy days of scalping ⅛ths and ¼ths were behind me. I had to change as well—but how? I had no real understanding of the markets. Charting, technical analysis, fundamentals, back testing—these were foreign concepts to me. Yet, as Albert Einstein reminded us, "In the middle of difficulty lies opportunity." So began my real development as a trader, as a student, and finally as a teacher.

That's why I am thrilled to be writing this foreword to *The Mentally Tough Online Trader*, by Bob Koppel.

As a veteran of almost 25 years trading and making markets, Bob is well known as the author of six books on the psychology of trading: *The Innergame of Trading; The Outer Game of Trading; Bulls, Bears, and Millionaires; The Intuitive Trader; The Tao of Trading;* and *The Market Savvy Investor*. He holds advanced degrees in Philosophy and Group Behavior from Columbia University. Best of all, Bob is that rare individual with a gift for life-changing insight, along with the ability to communicate that gift clearly.

In his latest book, *The Mentally Tough Online Trader*, he brings together a lifetime of trading, training, research, and hard-won experience. The result is an indispensable addition to the library of anyone who seeks to win in the market.

The foundation of all great trading lies within the trader himself. Bob's ability to gently force the reader to confront his *real* motivations for trading, and to articulate his deeply desired goals is central to building a truly strong foundation for trading. From that base, Bob skillfully helps the reader understand how to turn well-known psychological obstacles—anxiety, lack of confidence, lack of self-discipline—into powerful strengths.

For the past few years, I have been president of the most successful day trading firm in the country, Cornerstone Securities. While other day trading firms have generated, and then tried to avoid, the bad publicity that seems to plague the day trading industry, this firm has quietly and steadfastly built a model for the industry. No regulatory problems, no disgruntled customers, no press scandals. The most telling measure is that the overwhelming majority of its customers are consistently profitable.

How have they done it? Don't we hear everyday that "you can't make money as a short-term trader?" The answer is in *tools* and *education*. With an almost maniacal concentration on nurturing profitable traders, they have pioneered innovative training programs, effective trading techniques, and powerful trading tools.

These remarkable traders can no longer simply be called "day traders." They are on the leading edge of trading itself. They are daily pushing the envelop of trading possibilities. They are online traders—the embodiment of the Sixth Market, which is the term now being used to describe the electronic trading of securities by the self-directed individual.

The achievements of these leading traders have helped us to understand more clearly what it takes for anyone to succeed in the market. They have shown that it is no longer enough to be bright, competitive, or quick-reacting. They have shown that an educated understanding of the markets, skill in risk and capital management, psychological honesty and self-awareness, and adherence to a trading plan are even more important.

They have shown that great traders are made, not born.

Recently I resigned from Cornerstone to further my work in the education of traders—to spread this message, if you will. With more and more people entering the markets each day, the need for the effective education of market participants is acute, and Bob Koppel has proven to be among the best in the world at this task.

Let me be blunt: anyone who desires to trade, and who ignores the lessons in *The Mentally Tough Online Trader*, does so at great peril. In short, this book will give you the real *power* and *control* that you need to prosper in the markets.

Good Trading!

Kenneth R. Johnson, CEO
sixthmarket.com™

Preface

On July 29, 1999, Mark Barton, an Atlanta day trader, reportedly lost $150,000 in the stock market and bounced a $50,000 check put up for additional margin. He then went on a shooting rampage that resulted in the deaths of nine people killed at two office sites. The deaths raised serious questions about high-risk trading in a booming Wall Street bull market and the emotional upheavals for investors, many of whom are not prepared for the pressure or inevitable losses.

While authorities agreed that these were clearly the actions of a disturbed individual with a history of antisocial behavior, it was also generally accepted that his deadly outburst was triggered by huge losses in the market. A media frenzy ensued with a primary suspect in the glaring light of public scrutiny: day trading—the buying and selling of stocks faster than you can say "the mentally tough online trader."

The image of twenty-somethings using their computers to effect stock trades that result in the purchase of million dollar homes featuring garages stocked with BMWs fostered a perilous illusion: Wall Street's canyons were filled with gold for the taking. Added to this was the belief held by many traders and investors that now—armed with online technologies—the "old" ways of building wealth were replaced by a new era, a revolution in investing, requiring little more than a computer with a modem and simple software.

This is a world of trading that is faster, cheaper, and smarter than its predecessor. It is where, as an E*Trade publication states, "the financial planet is more evolved than ever before." Of course this point of view is in part correct, but it is not without its pitfalls.

Beyond the technology of computer power that surpasses the Starship Enterprise and the buzz and hoopla of financial information and resources never before available right at your fingertips, is the all-important psychological framework of the investor. To succeed at investing, like anything else, requires enormous discipline. One must establish a goal; adopt a personal course of action; and finally take action on a consistent basis, making the necessary adjustments and refinements as conditions and experience deem appropriate. It is effective action that produces results, which ultimately assures success. Ironically, while we live in the information age, information alone is not enough. How we communicate with ourselves determines how much of what we know we will use as investors and as human beings.

In the days after the Atlanta tragedy I was called by reporters and producers eager to learn more about the emotional impact and volatility of the online experience for investors: What are the psychological problems that come up for traders not properly trained to handle the wild swings and risks of the stock market?

I was both surprised and impressed with the media's level of interest and understanding of what is generally considered to be the "soft" side of Wall Street. I gave interviews to *The Wall Street Journal, Christian Science Monitor,* and *Boston Globe;* CBS radio; WLS, CNBC, and MSNBC television. They all wanted insight into the following questions:

- What emotional impact does online trading and investing have on its participants?
- What is the appropriate trading psychology for today's investor?
- What are effective trading tactics and strategies?
- How does one prepare for the inevitable risks and stresses of online trading?
- How does one seriously answer SEC chairman Arthur Levitt's concerns that today's new online investors are venturing into deep waters without proper education and the necessary background to protect them from harm?

Online trading can be safe and profitable. It is tested daily by millions of intelligent, hard-nosed, fair-minded critics—investors and traders like yourself. Whether you're an experienced trader or just starting out, this book is committed to giving you an edge to stay ahead of the curve. My aim is to help you invest with greater intelligence, understanding, discipline, and method—to give you the internal power and control to complement the technical capability of your computer and software.

There are more titles available today about the financial arena than ever before. Web sites are devoted to making it easier for you to invest and track your portfolio, and services telling you how to decide when to buy or sell stocks, options, or mutual funds. Electronically executed trades are confirmed in a matter of seconds. You can review your holdings 24 hours a day, 7 days a week. The content of this book, however, is different.

The Mentally Tough Online Trader focuses on the specific internal elements within each of us that form the basis of how we communicate with ourselves: the ways and things we visualize, hear, and feel that determine the outcomes of our trading and investment decisions.

The great single truth behind successful trading is this: successful traders produce exactly the results they want through specific physical and mental actions. It's important to bear in mind the opposite is true as well. Losses too are the result of individual actions. Our results—good or bad—are *not* a matter of chance.

Through the prism of professionally recognized top traders and investors we get a unique glimpse of the internal terrain of consistent winners, how they overcome the barriers and frustrations that hold most people back. What keeps them going is not a love of the "high wire." They are not the daredevils of the financial world. What they possess is the ability to keep moving forward, with discipline and decision, undeterred by setbacks.

Finally, and most importantly, the kind of effective personal communication and mental toughness that characterizes successful trading and investing can be learned. Just as any other skill, however, this toughness requires daily and on-going commitment and conditioning. To borrow a metaphor from the great twentieth century philosopher, Martin Buber, this book is about a "thou" rather than an "it." It is designed to help *you* better understand *your* motivations and internal structures that effect *your* market analyses and operations. You can then make *it* (profitable investments) happen. In my experience, there is no other way.

Success in all your investments (and everything else).

Acknowledgments

I wish to thank the many traders, analysts, market makers, and experts—too many to name here—who generously shared their ideas and insights into the workings of their creative minds. In particular, I would like to recognize my friend and business partner, Howard Abell, for his inestimable contributions. I also would like to thank Mara Koppel for reading the original manuscript and for providing her fine suggestions, all of which were taken. Thanks also to Cindy Zigmund and the staff at Dearborn for their uncompromising support throughout this project.

Finally, I would like to thank my many readers, who once again make all my efforts worthwhile.

PART 1

Investing Online

1

Investing Online

It is not the same to talk of bulls as to be in the bullring.

—Spanish proverb

I know traders and trading. Most of my adult life has been spent making trades, either on an exchange floor, or now, in front of a computer terminal. I can still remember trades being placed on "the floor" on chalk boards with quote takers calling out numbers to price recorders. In boardrooms, actual boards rotated to reveal last trades made. This is a world long gone, when there was a milkman or paperboy delivering the evening edition on a Schwinn Zephyr.

Today it is "welcome to the exciting world of online investing," where trades are lightning fast, information is a click away, and "life has suddenly gotten a lot better." It is a world of real-time, up-to-the-second stock quotes. Anyone can obtain financial data that a few years ago was available only to market professionals supported by sophisticated research departments. Educational materials are free for the asking, and market analyses from many sources are just a click away. Along with this also comes a Pandora's box of financial pitfalls where tips, rumors, and unscrupulous huckstering abound. There are other drawbacks: online investors are often vulnerable to chatroom (aptly named) stock recommendations and rumors, unregulated market analysis, and solicitations by unethical individuals.

The NASD has a task force that monitors and actively pursues prosecution of this type of illegal manipulative strategy. Notwithstanding their efforts, abuse of investment information and attempts at market manipulation on the Internet are still rampant. According to Rod Davis in *What You Need to Know Before You Invest* (Barron's, 1999):

> Many online traders turn into speculators rather than investors simply because of the means in which they execute orders. This type of trading activity certainly characterizes much of the online investing being done today . . . If what you are looking for on the Internet is the stock that seems to be skyrocketing the fastest and the highest, you will be more likely to take that ride. You are very likely to be wrong about the timing of both your purchase and sale.

Of course, the most difficult question for any investor to answer about the stock market is when to buy and when to sell. There have been innumerable books written to answer this question, but a definitive answer is still forthcoming. What is clear is this: successful investing is the result of decision-making based on logic, research, and method—not on emotions. This is a simple maxim, but it is not easy to implement! Many people dismiss it as being simplistic, however successful investors support its truth.

Investing requires a great deal of self-discipline, or what I call mental toughness. This is much more than mere "will power" or what Henry James called "a great heave of the will." It is a psychological commitment to act in a way that permits you to achieve your investment goals consistently.

Investors' attitudes toward their investments are profoundly influenced by online investing. Remember the technology itself is regularly characterized as exciting, and the truth be told, it is. Where you have *power* and *control*, investing is less a planned process than an event! The key point here is that if you have capital to invest, there is a compelling reason to take advantage of the opportunities offered in the securities market if approached with a desire to study and be involved in your trading decisions. That means, in most cases, learning more about yourself and the influences and impacts of the market on your emotions. I take it as an axiom that people are much too nervous and emotional when it comes to their money! (For a complete discussion of the psychology of money I would refer you to *Money Talks*, Dearborn, 1998.)

In Bernard Baruch's autobiography, *Baruch: My Own Story* (Holt, Rinehart & Winston, 1957), the legendary entrepreneur offers ten rules for successful investing. They are:

1. Don't speculate unless you do it full-time.
2. Resist so-called inside information and tips.
3. Before purchasing a security, know everything you can about a company: its earnings and capacity for growth.
4. Never attempt to buy a bottom or sell a top of a market. "This is a feat only achieved by liars."
5. Take your losses swiftly and clearly. The first loss is your easiest loss.
6. Don't buy too many securities. Focus on a few investments that can be monitored carefully.
7. Periodically reappraise all your investments to make sure they are appropriate to your particular strategy.
8. Know when you can sell to your greatest advantage (of course that also applies to buying).
9. Never invest all your funds. Keep some liquid.
10. Don't try to be a "jack of all investments." Stick to the field you know best.

Baruch, who was a life-long skeptic of both giving and receiving advice, qualified his rules of sound investment with this caveat: "Being so skeptical about the usefulness of advice, I have been reluctant to lay down any rules or guidelines on how to invest or speculate wisely. Still, there are a number of things I have learned from my own expense that might be worth listing for those who are able to muster the necessary self-discipline."

THE ONLINE EXPLOSION

Every minute of every day, thousands of investors around the world are opening online trading accounts. Consider the following statistics:

- The Internet accepts 1.5 million new users each month, a new user every 1.8 seconds. By 2002, half of all U.S. households will be online (McKinsey & Co.).
- The impact of the Internet on share trading is extensive, with volume growing exponentially. While percentages vary, some analysts estimate it accounts for as much as 25 percent of all stock trading activity in the United States.
- More than six million people have already traded online *(PC World)* and Charles Schwab claims it serves more than five million Internet investor accounts globally.
- Forrester research predicts that by 2003, 9.7 million U.S. households will manage more than $3 trillion in online investments in 20.4 million online accounts (Forrester, 1999).
- In 1998, 27 percent of all retail securities trades were made from computers (Piper Jaffray).
- More than 95 percent of individual investors surveyed in 1998 were satisfied with the quality of online trading (American Association of Individual Investors).
- McKinsey & Co. predicts that revenues from online personal financial services such as banking, credit cards, mortgages, and auto loans will spike dramatically in the next three years, with $400 billion in revenues likely to be generated from financial services by 2002. 58 percent could come from people who have online access. That opportunity is likely to intensify the battle between traditional banks, investment firms like Merrill Lynch, and start-ups like E*Trade.
- The next wave of online investors looks very different from "the young, curious, affluent, restless" first wave. "The second wave looks more like middle America" (McKinsey & Co.).

It is clear that notwithstanding the pitfalls, the individual investor has been a beneficiary of the advent of the Internet for all of the reasons already mentioned.For most investors, however, there is a crucial piece that is still missing: creating the winner's state of mind for consistent positive results.

If you turn to almost any book on investing you will see some or all of the following trading rules:

- Buy low, sell high
- Manage your money well
- Don't overtrade
- Don't turn a profit into a loss
- The trend is your friend
- Learn how to use orders properly
- Don't add to a loser
- Take big profits
- Take small losses
- Don't get stubborn
- Avoid the crowd
- Buy the rumor, sell the facts
- Avoid fear and greed
- Trade liquid markets
- Don't buy or sell price alone
- Preserve capital
- The market is always right

There are other rules and market axioms of course; and almost everyone knows them. But the question remains: why are so few investors able to consistently apply these rules for positive effect? The answer, I believe, has less to do with understanding objective rules and portfolio models and more to do with subjective experience: How do we see, hear, and feel markets, and then relate that information to ourselves before we make a trade?

The key to success in markets is as true today as it was fifty years ago and, I assume, will be so fifty years into the future. It involves old-fashioned, time-proven approaches of monetary and emotional discipline: effective strategy, thoughtful research, and the ability to embrace risk. Most of all, success requires a desire to learn: a commitment to be well-informed, clearly focused, and psychologically prepared, no matter what the market offers.

The famed financial trader Leo Melamed expressed this same idea to me when I interviewed him for *The Innergame of Trading* (McGraw-Hill, 1993):

> There is much to being a successful trader and investor. There are many rules to be applied and many lessons to be learned. There must be a willingness and ability to learn, to comprehend fundamentals and statistics, to grasp technical applications, to develop an inner trading sense, to accept defeat and live with victory, and much more. But most of all, there must be present a multitude of inborn characteristics relating to the trader's personality, psychology, emotional equilibrium, courage and patience.

Historically, books on investing have assumed psychological skills to be innate, that investors either possess or lack the ability and "nerve" to trade successfully. There is some merit to this idea in that some investors are clearly not suited to trade for either or both financial or psychological reasons. Their temperament, disposition, or attitudes make them ill-suited to invest on their own. For some this presents a considerable conflict given the current landscape of the investor revolution, where an investor is advised online, in print, and on TV to take one's own financial destinies firmly into one's own hands: to chart the waters of one's own fortunes, independent of the advice and explanations of financial planners, brokers, advisors, and market analysts.

Consider just a few of the current advertising campaigns, replaying many times each day on radio, television, and online.

- A Suretrade advertisement presents a series of very hip, good looking, well tailored men and women who, against a visually compelling backdrop, state: "we read, we learn, we

don't have blind faith, we're not relying on anyone else, we plan to retire rich, we're betting on ourselves, we are modern day capitalist mavericks."
- Ameritrade advises: "Believe in yourself."
- Another brokerage shows a glass wall separating online investors from the exchange floor. Suddenly the wall of glass shatters bringing the once rarefied world of professional trading into the reach of each of us.
- An online broker tells investors "Express yourself."

The message here is clear: Almost anyone can compete with the professionals using powerful computers with new software; cheaper telephone service; regulatory changes; the advent of online brokerage services; dirt cheap commissions; and access to free charts, quotes, high quality analysis products, and other resources. Wall Street's playing field has been democratized, leveled for the independent go-getter. An Ameritrade ad states: "Online trading: it satisfies on a molecular level."

How did we get here? What are the psychological implications for the online investor? Additionally, how is the individual investor to make sense of a stock market environment that is mutating so rapidly that no one can accurately predict what it will look like tomorrow.

Trading Evolution

Until the 1970s, the securities industry was conducted in its own time-honored fashion. The brokerage houses controlled the flow of orders, made largely to the New York Stock Exchange (NYSE) and to a lessor degree to the American Stock Exchange (AMEX) and the over-the-counter market (OTC). Not only was the order flow controlled, but the commissions charged to the general public were fixed. Price reporting was available at a broker's office or in newspapers, and only professional securities traders or wealthy individuals had access to real-time price and volume information.

9

In 1971 the National Association of Securities Dealers created Nasdaq, an electronic market where members could display their bids and offers to other members. On May 1, 1975, fixed commissions were terminated by a Securities and Exchange Commission (SEC) decree and a new era of competitive pricing and discount brokerage was born. The termination of fixed commissions, which was the culmination of a five-year phaseout and said at the time to be the death knell of the securities industry, actually turned out to be the main ingredient in the subsequent explosion of trading volume. An industry that had predicted brokerage house failures and the end of the industry saw a new breed of brokerage house called "discount brokers" provide an increased order flow at greatly reduced prices. Not only were discount brokers profitable, but they generated the explosion in trading volume by making the cost of buying and selling an insignificant factor for the investor.

Over the years, and with some SEC rule changes, the Nasdaq system has evolved from a member only, inside market to a quotation platform open to all. In 1985 the Small Order Execution System (SOES) was introduced to allow customers to buy on the offer and sell on the bid for up to one thousand shares at a time. After the 1987 crash, when market makers refused to answer phones or backed away from their quotes, Nasdaq instituted an automated electronic execution system through SOES. Soon after, the SelectNet System was created. It allowed investors to see and trade with market maker bids and offers as well as other customer's bids and offers.

The final ingredient in the explosion in the securities industry was and is the technological advances: online access to the markets that is readily available to all at a cheap cost with state-of-the-art quickness and precision. This technology offers the buying and selling of securities via the Internet, completely bypassing a broker as well as securing inexpensive online systems. As already mentioned, these online systems supply quotes, analyses and news, and allow for the direct entry of orders through participation on the SelectNet system and the various electronic communication networks (ECNs) that present investors' bids and offers on an equal footing with market professionals.

CHARACTERISTICS OF SUCCESSFUL INVESTORS

Despite—or maybe because of—the newly leveled playing field, investors are more conscious now than ever before of the importance of mastering specific psychological and tactical skills that are required to compete effectively as an online investor. Many individuals have come to realize that success is not about beating the street or the market, but rather about overcoming their own psychological and emotional biases that make them unwilling captives of the market's unpredictable and volatile nature.

Dickson G. Watts, a highly successful trader from an earlier generation, observed that "those who make for themselves an infallible plan delude themselves and others. Our effort will be to set forth the great underlying principle, the application of which must depend on circumstances, the times and the man." Watts identified five qualities that he believed were the essential characteristics of a successful investor.

1. *Self-reliance.* Independence of thought, conviction, and action where self-trust is the bedrock of one's efforts.
2. *Judgment.* To have an objective, honest view of the market where one understands one's natural inclination to have feelings of fear and greed.
3. *Courage.* Confidence based on competence. To be decisive, automatic, and resourceful. To trade in a state of mind that assures success.
4. *Prudence.* To have the ability to accurately define risk; to calculate and plan; and to develop strategies that consistently work.
5. *Pliability.* To be flexible, resilient, and open-minded. To have the ability to change an opinion.

When conducting training workshops with my business partner, Howard Abell, we would routinely ask the new traders, "what are the personal characteristics of successful traders?" Their responses often mirrored the list of personal characteristics that follow:

knowledgeable	high-achieving	stress managing
confident	open-minded	proactive
disciplined	determined	enjoys trading
self-reliant	optimistic	manages risk
motivated	intuitive	focused
competent	honest	independent
self-aware	patient	ambitious
organized	hard-working	committed
goal-oriented	high-achieving	stress managing
self-contained	energetic	automatic
knowledgeable	objective	risk taking

We would then ask trainees if they could name a single investor or trader who possessed all of these qualities. Occasionally we would hear the names Warren Buffet, Peter Lynch, Paul Tudor Jones, George Soros, or Abby Cohen, but most traders thought there was no one person who possessed all of these personal characteristics.

What do you think? Is there any trader who possesses all of the above named characteristics and, if so, who is he or she? As you think about this I would like to suggest to you that you need look no further than the nearest mirror. Are you not convinced? Don't we all have these personal characteristics in different degrees and in different proportions? The point is, many possess the ability—though not necessarily the capability—to develop any and all of these personal characteristics to become more effective at trading or anything else. Dorothy Parker said, "We are all works in progress."

This is important because all trading success, I believe, evolves from the realization that it is through the development of personal characteristics and effective attitudes (e.g., discipline, confidence, patience) that one creates the capability to devise investment strategies and techniques that will allow for a positive trading result. In fact, it is my belief that at the most basic level all trading strategies are an attempt by the individual trader to develop an external method to allow for the realization of these personal characteristics.

Some of the world's top traders said they became successful at trading after a prolonged period of frustration, loss, and disappointment. Tony Saliba contemplated suicide, Pat Arbor quit the Board of Trade for a year, and Leo Melamed went broke three times. Their comebacks were not through a specific method or technical approach. Tony Saliba's response was typical: "I learned how to focus, to become disciplined, objective." Pat Arbor said, "I just put my nose to the grindstone and got more focused, confident, consistent, and hard-working." Jeffery Silverman said, "I was always a long-term trader but I had to learn how to give up 'the death wish of overtrading,' to become truly disciplined, to focus more on the long-term signal and less on the noise. By so doing I taught myself how to trade the market: to buy it when it had value and to sell it when it did not."

In another exercise I would ask traders to construct specific statements about exactly what, in their opinions, separates the best traders and investors in the world from everyone else. I think you will their list:

- Top traders understand their motives for trading.
- Top traders develop trading strategies that work for them because they fit their personalities.
- Top traders enjoy trading and make it effortless.
- Top traders work hard at developing their skills and maintaining a trading edge.
- Top traders trade with total confidence in themselves and their methodology.
- Top traders trade in a positive state of mind that allows them the flexibility to act automatically and know exactly what is the next right step to take.
- Top traders intuitively understand money management and risk control and know no single trade is worth not being able to trade tomorrow.

- Top traders have a strategy that works and the discipline to carry it forward.
- Top traders are independent minded and understand they are personally responsible for all their market decisions.
- Top traders understand the difference between loss and losing.
- Top traders understand the importance of acting with circumscribed risk in difficult times.
- Top traders know what drives markets and understand the difference between hope and fear.
- Top traders don't trade to please others.

As you look at this list, ask yourself this question: do you believe you possess these qualities and characteristics. Unless you strongly believe that you can develop them, you are certainly pursuing the wrong path. I am fond of saying, "Believing is seeing." If you don't see and feel yourself possessing these qualities, characteristics, and attitudes, you will not sustain the effort, commitment, and hard work that is required to achieve peak performance as a trader. As I pointed out in *The Innergame of Trading*, what you believe about yourself and the market will enhance or inhibit your performance with dramatic results. In *Unlimited Power* (Fawcett, 1986), Anthony Robbins writes, "Our beliefs about what we are and what we can be precisely determine what we will be. If we believe in magic, we'll live a magical life. If we believe our life is defined by narrow limits, we've suddenly made those limits real. What we believe to be true, what we believe is possible, becomes what's true, becomes what's possible."

Successful online trading and investing grows in the rich soil of hard work, discipline, and preparation. Becoming a mentally tough online trader requires an ongoing commitment to mastery over internal hindrances and fears. John R. Noe observes in *Peak Performing Principles for High Achievers*, (Berkeley, 1984), "Fear is the most powerfully inhibiting force known to man. It restricts us, tightens us, and causes us to panic, forcing us to abandon our great plans of life. If we are not willing to do what we fear, the fear, not ourselves, is in control of our lives. The high achiever cannot afford to surrender control of his or her life to fear."

To overcome fear you must face it head-on because if you don't control the fear, it will control you! I once heard Zig Ziglar define fear in a most memorable way. Ziglar said, "Fear is an acronym; it stands for *False Evidence Appearing Real*."

As you begin to think about the internal hindrances and fears that are keeping you from achieving the result you want in the stock market, ask yourself the following questions (Write down the answers):

- Do I really want to become a successful online trader? Why?
- Do I possess the internal skills necessary to succeed?
- Am I willing to pay the price of time and effort to succeed?
- What really matters most to me?
- Am I willing to assume responsibility for all my trading actions?
- Am I committed to start where I am?
- Am I capable of thinking for myself?
- Am I willing to live up to my full potential?

Consider this comment by Jack Sandner, another legendary trader, about what it takes to be a successful trader.

Some folks think traders have a nice life, based on the misbegotten notion that they breeze in at about 8:30 in the morning and are out the door and on the golf course or wherever by 4:00 in the afternoon. What they don't realize is how much happens before and after the opening and closing bells. Just as any trial lawyer worth his or her salt devotes many, many hours to preparation and strategy, so does any good trader. Preparing for those crucial hours on the trading floor entails an incredible amount of homework: no chart is ignored, no statistic, however esoteric it may seem, is discounted. Next, a precise strategy for the next day's trading must be mapped. That strategy must be so thorough that it will get the trader into the market at exactly the right point, define the trader's risk, and take the trader out at just the precise moment. Once involved in the market, it should all be a matter of focus and execution.

—Jack Sandner, "How Winning Traders Think," 1996

Learn to See Everything Accurately

"Think of what is right and true. Learn to see everything accurately. Become aware of what is not obvious. Be careful even in small matters. Do not do anything useless." This was the advice of Miyamoto Musashi in *The Book of the Five Rings* (1643). It is one of the most important Samurai texts ever written. Its strategic insights were designed for leaders in all professions who were searching for individual mastery and personal excellence.

The curious fact about Musashi's advice—and for that matter, all recommendations about successful trading practice—is that in a real and practical sense, strategy and technique must be learned only to be forgotten. It is not my intention to be cute when I say that. What I mean is that you must work hard at learning an effective market technique and strategy, but this is only a starting point. It is like becoming a jazz musician. You must spend countless hours practicing—doing scale work and fingering exercises. But when you are performing you must be prepared to let go and follow where the line takes you, to be immersed in the spirit and soul of the music. In other words, you must internalize the concepts and attitudes learned.

In *Zen and the Way of the Sword, Arming the Samurai Psyche* (Oxford, 1990), Winston L. King underscores this point, "The swordsman handles his sword as if he were handling chopsticks, picking up a piece of food and putting it into his mouth. . . . Everything must be turned over to the unconscious/subconscious visceral awareness. There is no room or time here for thought."

I believe Ed Seykota, a market wizard, made this same point when he was interviewed by Jack Schwager (*Market Wizards*, 1990). Seykota indicated there are five trading rules he lives by:

1. Cut losses.
2. Ride winners.
3. Keep bets small.
4. Follow the rules without question.
5. Know when to break the rules.

In the chapters that follow it is my intention to demonstrate how you can develop the psychological, emotional, and tactical skills necessary to become a successful online trader. It is my hope that, through practice and exercise, you will commit to internalize these concepts and attitudes so that they become "hard-wired" to your nervous system. Thus, your natural response to the dynamic slings and arrows of the market will be one of mental toughness based on preparation, discipline, calculated risk taking, and research. Let's now look at what kind of investor you are.

2

What Kind of Investor Are You?

The first rule of investing is a simple one: investor know thyself! The best way to accomplish this involves a significant responsibility— educating yourself. You must determine your own net worth in order to establish how much you have to invest. You must identify those factors that influence your approach to investing or trading. And then you must create a strategy that best suits your goals, methods, and personality.

There are more than nine thousand listed securities on the NYSE, ASE, and Nasdaq. You can purchase one stock or put together a portfolio of stocks. Or you can purchase mutual funds and put your money in the hands of a professional money manager. To secure larger returns from mutual funds requires sitting through several business cycles, exercising patience to stay invested for ten years or longer. The key to success is to pick a diversified growth fund that performed in the top quartile of all mutual funds over the last five years with a good track record over the last 12 months.

When thinking about being a mentally tough online trader one would not normally think this concept refers to a mutual fund owner, but in truth it does. Of course, most people considering online investing will naturally elect a more active involvement in their own investment portfolio. Consider for a moment, however, the most common mistakes made by people who purchase mutual funds who don't reap large returns:

- Failing to be patient for the required 10 to 15 years of investment
- Worrying about management fees, dividends paid, or turn-over rates
- Being affected by day to day news or having a short-term opinion rather than investing for the long term
- Selling out during a breaking market
- Losing confidence too soon

Fear and greed play themselves out constantly in the stock market. According to statistics, almost half the people invested in some of the best performing funds lose money because they are afraid to experience the natural ups and downs of the market. Investors in funds are subject to the same debilitating emotions as the individual trader and therefore need to develop their own brand of mental toughness.

Although we are reminded daily that investing in securities has never been easier or cheaper, making sound investment or trading decisions requires more than the click of a mouse. Cheap and easy does not equal successful trading or investing. Nothing substitutes for research and education.

LONG-TERM MARKET TRENDS

Although the focus of this book is the active online investor, it is important to remember that long-term investing in equities has paid off handsomely for the patient investor. The stock market has had a steady return on equity averaging about 10 percent annually. Since 1982 the U.S. stock market has had a bull market that has taken the Dow Jones Industrial Average of 30 stocks from under

800 points to more than 11,500 points 18 years later. A similar move was realized by the Standard and Poor's 500 Stock Index, which consists of some of the largest capitalized companies in the United States (see Figures 2.1 and 2.2). And of course, the Nasdaq has shattered all previous records (see Figure 2.3). This has been the longest bull market in U.S. history.

Economic conditions, inflation expectations, interest rates, government policies, and the productivity of workers in general guide the stock market. Individual companies must be viewed in the general context and then individually analyzed on the basis of specific market criteria.

Personally, I favor the long-term market approach of William J. O'Neil in his book, *How to Make Money in Stocks* (McGraw-Hill, 1995), for the long-term online investor. O'Neil's criteria for stock selection is contained in the acronym CANSLIM:

C = Current quarterly earnings per share.
A = Annual earnings increases: look for meaningful growth.
N = New products, new management, new highs.
S = Supply and demand: small capitalization plus volume demand.
L = Leader or laggard: which is your stock?
I = Institutional sponsorship: a little goes a long way.
M = Market direction: being able to determine it is essential to success.

The point here is that successful fundamental stock selection is focused on key factors: earnings growth, product development, and good management. All this information is readily available on-line through information services, brokerages, and libraries.

Common Investing Mistakes

As an active online trader, research, education, and method are equally critical for a positive result. Consider for a moment some of the most common mistakes investors fall prey to. You will read-

21

FIGURE 2.1   Long-Term Trend: Dow Jones

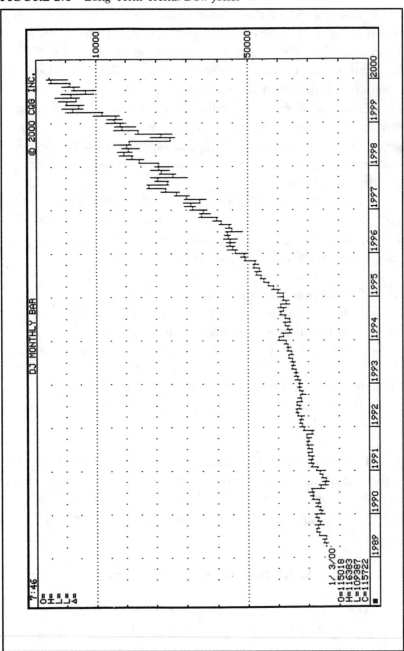

FIGURE 2.2 Long-Term Trend: S&P 500

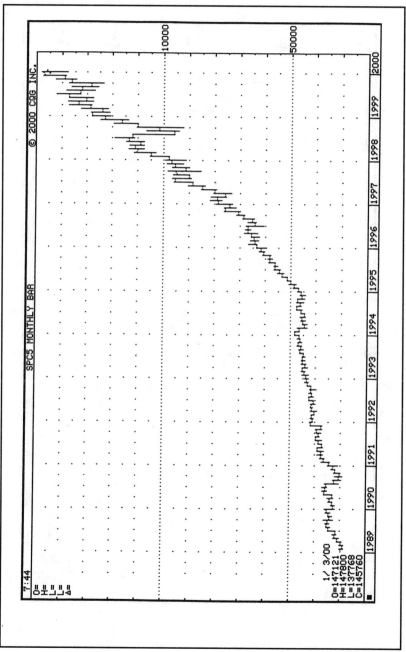

FIGURE 2.3 Long-Term Trend: Nasdaq

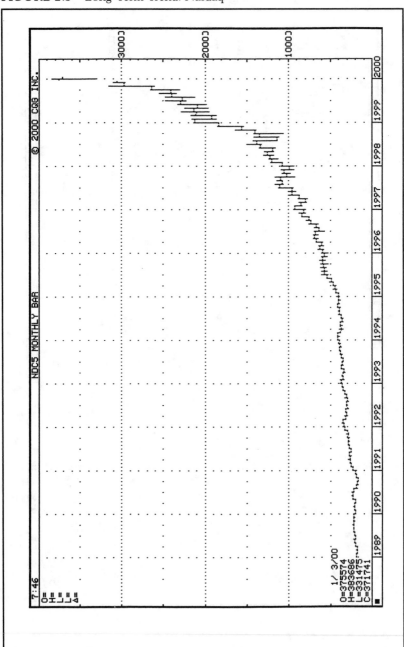

ily see how both long-term and short-term traders share common pitfalls:

- Poor stock selection based on performance and/or liquidity
- Bottom picking
- Averaging a loss
- Taking a chance on a cheap stock or "lowrisk" trade
- Trying to make a "killing"
- Buying a tip, rumor, or story
- Making a trading or investment decision based on a gut feeling rather than research
- Holding onto losses
- Taking profits too soon
- Focusing on commissions and fees rather than opportunities
- Holding out for a specific price rather than buying at the market in the direction of your analyzed market bias
- Getting caught up in a belief or opinion
- Vacillating whether to buy or sell at critical moments

MARKET STRATEGY

Now let me ask you some specific questions in order to help you assess your overall market strategy.

- How would you characterize your overall approach to the stock market?
- What unique strengths and weaknesses do you bring to your investment or trading decisions?
- What part of the investment process do you most enjoy (e.g., analysis, evaluation, long-term or short-term trading) about participating in the stock market?
- How much time are you willing to invest in research and education?
- What is your basic stock market philosophy?

25

- What specific beliefs or biases do you bring to the stock market that will inhibit or enhance your investing strategy?

Warren Buffett once said that he surely would have failed if he had tried to be a floor trader. He understood that in order to be effective he had to consider his unique strengths and weaknesses to function best in the stock market. As a long-term value-oriented, buy-and-hold investor he must be thoroughly conversant with a company's annual reports, management, quality of earnings, market dominance, and so on. It suits his market temperament and methods and in so doing, reflects his personality.

Short-term traders, on the other hand, rely on strategies that exploit market psychology that influences sudden and dramatic shifts in price action. They can read the market based on their unique "feel" (corroborated by indicators) of market tone and personality. Often they have little or no concern for the underlying market influences, long-term fundamentals, or technical analytical data. They have cultivated the ability and honed skills relying on specific information—conscious and subliminal—that is geared for their individual approaches. Mr. Buffett would have difficulty succeeding in such an environment. It is important to remember that ultimately, each investor can only succeed by knowing an individual game plan and exercising it with decision and discipline. Each must employ research relevant to a trading style in order to be effective and secure a profitable result. To be successful you must identify a strategy and time frame that works for you.

BASIC TRADING STRATEGIES

There are only a few basic strategies employed by online traders. They range from long-term investing, as mentioned above, to very short-term market scalping (capturing small price increments). For each to be successful, trading decisions must be careful, methodical, researched, and well thought-out. For purposes of describing appropriate goals and time frames within a given investment horizon, there are five categories of online traders:

1. Long-term investor
2. Long-term trader
3. Swing trader
4. Day trader
5. Options trader

Long-Term Investor

The long-term investor's time frame is a minimum of one year and may extend out for many years. His or her trading decisions are based on a well-formulated calculation based on fundamental and technical factors that affect stock market prices. Portfolios may be diversified, invested in specific funds or sectors, or concentrated in single issues. In addition to some of the stock selection criteria already mentioned, the long-term investor may take some or all of the following into consideration:

Securities ratios

- Price-earnings ratio
- Dividend payout
- Book value per share
- Price to book ratio

Measurements of profitability

- Earnings per share
- Profit margin
- Return on equity
- Total return (stock): capital appreciation plus dividends
- Total return (mutual funds): change in net asset value plus capital gains plus income distributions

Measurements of leverage

- Debt to asset ratio
- Debt to equity ratio

Measurements of liquidity

- Working capital
- Current ratio: assets divided by current liabilities
- Acid-test ratio: current assets minus inventories divided by current liabilities

Measurements of activity

- Inventory turnover ratio
- Accounts receivable turnover
- Total asset turnover

For the long-term investor, the numbers provide a means of identifying an undervalued company or fund before the rest of the market gets wind of an impending opportunity. Bear in mind, some stocks do not lend themselves to the strict use of the criteria in each category cited above. An example of how a long-term investor would use information to analyze a stock such as Microsoft is as follows: The investor would first look at Microsoft's price-earnings ratio and compare it with similar companies, taking into consideration Microsoft's income and sales figures for the previous 12 months and its percentage changes. The investor would also factor in the net profit margin and how much debt Microsoft holds, comparing that to its overall equity. She or he would then look at the stock price change in the last 3, 6, and 12 month periods and compare it with similar companies (e.g., Sun Microsystems) in the industry. Finally, the investor would analyze how the stock has performed compared to the broader market (its relative strength).

Long-Term Trader

The long-term trader's time horizon may extend from a week to a year. He or she is focusing on many of the same factors that the long-term investor is considering. In addition, this trader is relying on technical indicators and indices to initiate market entry and exit strategies. Long-term traders will stay with their positions until market dynamics have aligned measurably, targeted price levels have been reached, or fundamental conditions have changed.

Swing Trader

The swing trader's focus is generally three to five days. She or he seeks to identify pivotal points in the stock market's weekly actions, searching for entry points based on perceived buying and selling climaxes, price retracements, trendline pullbacks, and the like. (These terms will be described in detail in Part 4.) Risk parameters are highly calculated and well-defined. The swing trader seeks to exploit critical turns in the market or in particular issues that may materialize into larger stock market moves.

Day Trader

On the floor of financial exchanges, "scalpers" move in and out of markets with surgical precision, buying the bid and selling the offer to capture small price increments. In the stock market, their equivalent is the market maker. The market maker's focus is to make small profits by capturing an $\frac{1}{8}$ here, and a $\frac{1}{16}$ there, on each transaction. The market maker limits exposure by moving quickly with a closely defined risk to secure market "edge." Day traders, whether scalping the market or looking to capture larger ($\frac{1}{2}$ to 2 points per trade) moves, are utilizing a strategy based primarily on volume rather then price movement. Key to the day trader's success is lightning fast execution and complete focus on market entry and exit tactics and strategy. Day traders typically do not allow for the exposure of an open position overnight.

Options Trader

Options offer a very attractive avenue of investment because they present so many variable strategic possibilities. Specific strategy selection is based on considerations of price, timing, volatility, and direction. In addition, the trader must factor in risk/reward characteristics, expected returns, and percent of equity to invest. Strike prices and expirations can be selected to create a myriad of interesting market opportunities ranging from the day traders time horizon to that of the long-term investor. For a full discussion of options, please refer to Howard Abell's *The Electronic Trading of Options* (Dearborn, 2000).

The key to success in each category is knowing what you are looking *for* and looking *at* in the stock market. You must know the characteristics of your time frame and then adopt a strategy that is appropriate to it. Many traders make the mistake of trading within a particular time horizon, only to switch their perspective midstream. Mental toughness means you stay focused and disciplined within your own strategy, understanding what it takes to be successful within its investment parameters, and then acting accordingly. As one top trader explained, "A huge challenge for most traders is being able to achieve consistency. If you want to succeed, you've got to be consistent."

But how do you achieve consistency? The answer is by rigorously following your investment system and abiding by your research and market-tested strategies that have proven over time to work. This is difficult for most investors who have a strategy all worked out in their minds but allow momentary feelings or thoughts to dictate their stock market decisions.

It is important to underscore these key points, which I believe apply to all traders and investors and ultimately allow you to be a mentally tough market participant.

- *Be patient.* Wait for stock market opportunities to materialize based on your well-thought-out and researched game plan.
- *Stay disciplined.* See the big picture unfold. Even if you are a day trader, know what *your* big picture is! It is being consistent with your overall risk and money management parameters within the borders of your time frame.
- *Be strategic.* Have a trading plan that limits losses and lets profit run.
- *Be an expert in your market.* Know the characteristics of the issues you are trading. Do the necessary fundamental and technical analysis that is required.
- *Have clearly defined goals.*
- *Exercise strict risk control.* Maintain highly controlled risk/reward ratios.
- *Be in a optimum trader's state of mind.* Be positive and resourceful, with a high degree of focus. All the preparation and discipline will make you relaxed and confident.

Now ask yourself, again, the following questions:

- Do I really want to become a mentally tough online trader?
- Do I possess the skills necessary to succeed?
- Am I willing to pay the price?
- Am I willing to assume personal responsibility for all my market actions?
- Am I willing to start from where I am?
- Am I willing to think for myself?
- Am I committed to living up to my full potential?

I would like to close this chapter with a quote from George Leonard's book, *Mastery* (Dutton, 1991): "To take the master's journey, you have to practice diligently, striving to hone your skills, to attain new levels of competence. But while doing so—and this is the inexorable part of the journey—you also have to be willing to spend most of your time on a plateau, to keep practicing even when you seem to be getting nowhere."

This is a profound statement that has been repeated many times to me by some the world's top traders and market professionals. It is the burning desire to achieve mastery that ultimately produces success. In *The Mental Game* (Viking Penguin, 1990), James Loehr writes, "Desire was consistently identified as the chief factor leading to competitive success." This too has been my observation. Given the broad range of stock market strategies that can be successful, it is the investor's attitudes, beliefs, and discipline that ultimately yield results. Courage and positive attitudes combined with sound stock market principles and methods will, in time, result in the desired outcome. Your persistence and determination to succeed is, in the final analysis, the critical element.

Psychological Skills of the Online Trader

3

Motivation

Two hemispheres of the brain are better—
and more profitable than one.

—*Bennett W. Goodspeed*
The Tao Jones Averages

Let us look now at the specific psychological skills necessary to become a mentally tough online trader. It is my goal here to identify each skill set so that it can be learned and practiced with specific exercises to help you experience the often promised "control" and "power" of online trading. Based on many years of battle-forged trading experience, training my own proprietary traders, and interviewing hundreds of the world's most successful traders, I have identified six trading assumptions you must follow:

1. Security prices are not random. There is an underlying order to all markets and price action.
2. Effective trading and investing can be taught.
3. The psychological side of investment is key.
4. The investor's state of mind, focus, and personal belief system will be the determining factors for success, not a particular portfolio model or trading system.
5. Investing discipline produces confidence.
6. You must understand and act on your motives and goals for trading and investing in order to achieve a positive result.

THE PSYCHOLOGICAL SKILLS OF THE MENTALLY TOUGH ONLINE TRADER

- Compelling motivation
- Goal setting
- Confidence
- Anxiety control
- Focus
- State management
- Positive and empowering imagery
- Ongoing mental conditioning

As you review this list, consider how each of these skills—when optimized—would improve your online trading experience. Let's first look at the importance of motive and motivation for the online trader.

Motivating Yourself

To motivate yourself to accomplish any goal you must first identify your motives and then take action on them. It is, therefore, critical that you understand your motives for trading. So, let me begin by asking you a very simple question: Why do you want to trade?

As you analyze your motives for trading, ask yourself if it is essential for you to trade online in order to satisfy your motives. For example, if your motive is excitement ("welcome to the exciting world of online trading"), can you satisfy this need by hang gliding or windsurfing? If the answer is yes, stop reading here! If, however, you have a burning, insatiable appetite to become a successful online trader, you should learn as much as possible about yourself and the equities markets.

Think for a moment about anything that you ever did or accomplished in your life that you truly enjoyed. Get a clear picture of it in your mind. It makes no difference if it was an intellectual or physical activity. Consider how important your level of motivation was to your ultimate success.

Once you are aware of your motives for trading online, you will realize how the strength of your motives dictate the intent and intensity of any course of action that you will adopt in the market. If your core motive, for example, is the intrinsic intellectual challenge of beating the market, then choosing a personal trading style and strategy that consciously builds into it the awareness of this motive will help determine your optimum market behavior. Put simply, motive dictates how and on what you focus, the level of confidence and esteem you experience, the efficacy or limitation of personal beliefs (as they relate to trading), and the degree to which your state of mind is positive and resourceful—all the necessary ingredients for successful online trading.

The following is a visual representation of the importance of understanding motive for successful trading.

Motive → Focus → Personal Market Strategy

Motive guides focus, which results in an individual's ultimate market strategy.

SOME COMMON REASONS FOR TRADING ONLINE

- Excitement
- Get rich quick
- Entertainment
- It's cool

Excitement

Trading online is, in fact, very exciting. But trading online for excitement is not a good reason to participate in the stock market.

For many traders, this kind of trading becomes akin to purchasing a lottery ticket. Each action is motivated by an energizing and electric fantasy. The online TV commercials play to this type of thinking all day long: online trading equals big houses, yachts, trips to Caribbean islands, and sparkling jewels.

Get Rich Quick

For investors, online trading becomes what the "Handy House-wife Helper" was for Ralph Kramden in the old "Honeymooners" series: a get rich quick scheme. Everybody's doing it, so can you! Wrong!

Entertainment

"Investors" who trade for entertainment find out very soon that they are playing a leading role in their own real life docudrama, where losses mount and show time is an all too expensive production! There are others who trade just so that they can inform their friends at parties, "I'm an online trader." I have known traders like that and am not surprised when I hear about their poor results. To be successful at online trading, investors need to know that they are engaged in serious business!

It's Cool

With ease of access, and hands-on control, online trading is a very "cool" thing to do, but doing it solely for that reason is not!

The best motive for trading online is because it is an intellectually stimulating, disciplined form of investing that allows you to capitalize on stock market opportunities. Decisions therefore are based on knowledge. And while "knowledge is power," the power comes from knowing what to do with the knowledge—identifying an opportunity and taking advantage of it with a sound investment strategy.

LESSONS OF THE TOP TRADERS

Top traders have not inherited a top-trading gene. Winners are not born, they are made. They think and act in ways that assure success.

The most compelling force in your development as a trader, or as a human being for that matter, is the thinking you engage in and the beliefs you possess about yourself and your environment. If you do not believe in failure and deny its reality, you cannot be defeated. The only real limitations on what you can accomplish are those you impose on yourself. It is important to remember that you are empowered to create your own reality. This is helpful information to possess. There can be no great success in trading without great commitment, hard work, discipline, and the realization of the "right" type of thinking.

Compelling motivation is possessing the intensity and knowledge to do whatever it takes to succeed at trading; to overcome past mistakes or setbacks in order to achieve your investment goals.

Think of the intensity and discipline of a world-class athlete; fully engaged and not afraid to play the game; not afraid of "being there," totally involved, motivated and prepared. A successful trade results from following specific steps.

A Successful Online Trading Decision

Well analyzed and → Automatic execution → Successful trading
strategized trade   (based on confidence)   result (independent
(based on research)   of actual profitability
                                                  of any one trade)

Motivation by Winners

Compelling motivation is a common characteristic among the top traders who I have interviewed. Consider just a few comments that illustrate this point. Leo Melamed summed it up this way:

From the moment I entered the trading scene and opened the door to this arcane world of shouting and gesticulations, I was bewitched. The tumult; the color; the frenzy of activity; the people rushing about, shouting at the top of their voices; and acting out their mysterious incantations instantly inflamed my young and unworldly soul, awakened some unknown and uncontrollable passions from deep within, and caused me to irrevocably conclude that this, whatever it was, was for me. And so it came to pass. Although I finished law school and even successfully practiced law for some six or seven years, my heart, mind, and soul never left the world of trading.

Another trader, Joel Greenberg, said:

Once I discovered what was involved in trading, it became an intriguing situation because of supply and demand characteristics. Once you got into a given market, it became a mystery to solve . . . not a mystery of something that's happened in the past, but a mystery of what was going to happen in the future. Since I've been a child, I've loved to put jigsaw puzzles together. The same thing holds true for the market. The idea that I would begin to talk to certain individuals who all had the same information that I had. It was interesting to hear that two or three individuals looked at it one way and someone else looked at it another way. The way the best people looked at the market was to try and put in as many variables that the other people weren't thinking about, to come up with where they thought the market was going to go. For me trading is all about the mystery of trying to figure out where the markets are going, just like a puzzle.

For Joseph Siegel:

It was the challenge that attracted me to trading. I realized soon enough that trading is a game where you're going to have to compete and you better equip yourself to be able to compete aggressively with self-confidence and nerve. I loved the idea of competition, watching the eyes and overall movement of the different traders . . . learning to understand how they would react in advance and then beating them to the punch.

When I asked Gene Agatstein what first attracted him to trading, he said:

I was a teenager and I saw a pretty lively over-the-counter stock market. I had a summer job with a firm and I was really impressed with how much fun everybody was having. The closest thing that I had seen to trading up until that time was sporting events, athletic encounters with winners and losers. That really appealed to me. Especially when I saw the political nature of the alternative jobs that came along. I think I was running away from politics, perhaps even away from human interaction. What really first attracted me to trading was the sense of independence and fun and the pure meritocratic nature of trading. You are either right or wrong and you know right away. This really appealed to me.

4

Setting Goals

Setting goals is imperative for the trader to enhance motivation and optimize performance. Goals should be realistic and measurable, within one's control, and realized within a specific time frame. By setting goals, the online trader conditions himself or herself to boost trading to the next level of competence. It is excellence—not perfection—that is the point here. Seeking excellence produces results; seeking perfection produces ulcers!

There is an anecdote that is told of H. L. Mencken that on a particularly quiet day in an otherwise noisy newsroom, Mencken began to shout at the top of his lungs, "It's coming in the doors, we must stop it!" Needless to say, everyone stopped what they were doing and began looking in his direction. "It's up to the bottom of the desks!" yelled Mencken and then he shouted again, "It's up to the seats of our chairs!"

Mencken's colleagues began to look at one another. Seeing no observable threat, they began to mutter among themselves, "What is he talking about?" In a final grand gesture, Mencken jumped on top of his desk and bellowed, "Mediocrity! We're drowning in mediocrity!"

Commitment to hard work and self-improvement may seem to be an obvious point. In realty, I believe it's the essential point. It is what provides the personal propulsion toward excellence and the means with which we grow to learn more about ourselves and the market. Commitment is the psychic fuel that allows us to face our fears, to realize we cannot escape them, and that to face them is to overcome them. The importance of this lies in the all-too-familiar saw that the power of fear is amplified by fear itself. If we don't confront our fears in trading or anything else, what results is an experience that is based on intimidation, wasted potential, and pessimism.

To overcome the fear (e.g., executing trades confidently) you must face it head on. Setting goals is an important first step.

There is an old *New Yorker* cartoon where two guys are sitting in their totally trashed Manhattan apartment. They are unshaven and unkempt, newspapers and takeout cartons and wrappers everywhere. There is a smokey disorderly haze hanging all around them. Suddenly, one turns to the other and says: "This is ridiculous, let's get this place organized next month."

Becoming a mentally tough online trader requires a commitment to learn, and like making any other significant change in your life, requires that certain specific conditions are met. They are:

- Know your outcome
- Develop a plan of action
- Reevaluate and retool

KNOW YOUR OUTCOME

The online trader must have a specific goal in mind. It is therefore important that you know exactly, in detail, what mechanical or psychological skill, market technique, or strategy; risk management algorithm; or online trading style you want to master. You must be able to know when you have accomplished your goal in quantifiable and verifiable terms.

DEVELOP A PLAN OF ACTION

The online trader must develop a program, that is a personal strategy to accomplish a specific end, based on homework, hard work, and discipline. No short cuts here!

REEVALUATE AND RETOOL

The world of the online trader is, as you know by now, both exciting and fraught with risk, unpredictability, and volatility. It is a world that incubates ambiguity and requires, to borrow a word coined by Timothy Gallwey, the author of *The Inner Game of Tennis,* "unfreakability." Although writing about the psychological aspects of tennis, Gallwey's observation is equally appropriate for the online trader. "Unfreakability refers not to our propensity for burying our head in the sand at the sight of danger, but to see the true nature of what is happening and to be able to respond appropriately. This requires a mind that is clear because it is calm."

If you want to succeed at online trading, it must be viewed as a process, not an event. It requires nothing less than the ability to easily adjust to changing market conditions. When ideas or strategies work, use them. When they don't work, discard them and move on. Successful online trading requires the sensory and intellectual acuity to discern between winning and losing strategies and to act accordingly. The key point here is you need flexibility, knowledge, and persistence.

WHAT ALL TRADERS SHARE
IN COMMON

All traders, from the novice to the professional market maker, have certain things in common: they take losses, get frustrated, experience stress, and go through periods—sometimes extended—of drawdowns and disappointment. But the top traders, at varying points in their careers, undertook to develop personal strategies for overcoming setbacks. They taught themselves specific, personal methods of getting around potentially disabling psychological impediments.

Consider the comments of Hawksbill Capital Management CEO, Tom Shanks, when I asked him how he personally dealt with periods of poor or negative performance:

> I think anybody that goes through a drawdown questions whether what he's doing is correct and whether the systems are still viable, so there's a real struggle with that. For me, experiencing a drawdown is a tremendous motivation to get back on track. There's a reassurance that when you get back to analyzing things and realize that drawdowns happen, you tell yourself that ultimately you will come out of it. It's obviously very hard on the client and your own state of mind, but it's part of the whole process. You've got to take care of yourself on a personal level, make sure you're getting enough rest and exercise and that kind of thing. Make sure you're bringing enough energy to the effort. So there's a lot of personal management involved as well.
>
> You can't kid yourself in trading. You have to deal with who you really are, and take responsibility for all your shortcomings that the markets have a way of revealing rather starkly. You have to confront all your fears and tame them. You have to check your ego at the door.
>
> You learn from each experience. There's nothing in life that you can do that can guarantee that you're not going to go through some pain. Trading is certainly not a singular pursuit in that regard. What I have learned is this: patience and diligence are rewarded. Profits will eventually accrue if you do the right thing and stick with it. That's the most important thing!

Bryan Gindof, a successful screenwriter and former president of Del Rey Investment Management, offered this insightful comment about the similarity of Wall Street and Hollywood and what trading ultimately taught him about himself:

> On Wall Street, just like in Hollywood, you want to look for a very strong story that's so powerful that it can succeed in spite of what might not be great execution, and if you can find great execution to go along with it, then you really hit the jackpot. For instance, in the last five years, one of the strongest stories has been computer networking stocks. About five years ago, if you looked at the world and said, "Hey, there are all these zillions of computers out there and somehow they're all going to have to get tied together so they can communicate with each other," well, you had an incredibly strong story there.
>
> So then if you went looking in the networking sector for stocks to buy, as opposed to other sectors of the market, you dramatically increased your probability of making a much higher return on your money. There's a good chance that you could have done quite well for a while just buying a large basket of networking stocks because the market was recognizing the strength of the basic idea and carrying poor to average companies along for the ride with the very good companies. You see that all the time in the market.
>
> And if you went the next step and identified the leaders—Cisco, Cabletron, 3 Com, for instance—then you really did make tons of money. Essentially those were the companies that not only had the compelling story idea, but they also executed it with great dialogue and a great cast. I think there really is a good analogy between how you make money in the movie business and how you make money in the market. Movie studios make their big money from blockbusters, which are often referred to as "tentpoles," the films that hold up the tent, so to speak. Generally, if you're going to have a shot at making outsized returns in a portfolio, you need a few tentpole stocks—core holdings where you concentrate more of your money because you've found a company or a few companies with compelling stories, and, hopefully, great execution too. In both

47

arenas I believe the biggest money is almost always made when you can tap into the compelling themes . . .

I think trading has taught me a lot about myself. As a matter of fact, I think the whole process, if you allow yourself to really be open, is like going through psychotherapy every day. It really gives you an opportunity to see what you're all about.

The market forces you, if you're going to succeed, to be completely honest with yourself. If you're losing money, you are simply forced to confront that reality. It's an objective reality, it's right in front of you and you have to acknowledge it. Truthfully, I believe the market weeds out people who are unable to be honest with themselves. I suspect that trading, aside from being a fascinating way to make a living, is also one of the most self-revelatory things that a person can do. Day in and day out you're confronted with all your primal emotions.

Choosing to become a mentally tough online trader, in psychological terms, is not very different from adopting any significant change in your life. It requires what I call the four Cs of top trading.

THE FOUR Cs OF TOP TRADING

1. Commitment
2. Conviction
3. Constructing new patterns of behavior
4. Conditioning

Commitment

All significant change begins, as discussed earlier, with a strong overriding motivation to succeed. Picture the intensity of Michael Jordan, Tiger Woods, Andre Agassi, or Florence Griffith-Joyner. Top performing traders are committed to overcome any hardship or roadblock to achieve their goals. They are not afraid to play the game—even when they know they might take losses. Tom Grossman is president of SAC International Equities, LLC. He was formerly the head foreign equities trading strategist for Kingdon Capital Management, a billion-dollar hedge fund. Consider his personal approach to investing:

> In high school I played football and lacrosse and I was also a swimmer. In college I concentrated exclusively on football. I certainly think the competitive element, the discipline involved in succeeding at sports, spills over to most occupations, but trading particularly . . .
>
> Early in my career at Kingdon, the Japanese equity market was extremely weak. The Nikkei had broken 15,000 and everyone in the world was bearish. I started to feel on a purely intuitive basis and then later on a more quantitative basis that the market was ready to take off and I built a case for a long position in what was a very illiquid, difficult market to trade. The result however, was that I picked the bottom of the market and had an extremely profitable trade! And I think that defines my confidence in my own intuition and investment process. You must have the courage of your own convictions to buck the trend and act on your own intuitive beliefs.
>
> I find you have to recognize when you have an advantage. If you're not sitting with a position in a market that's getting killed, that's a tremendous advantage because you don't have the emotional pain that everyone else is experiencing. It's almost your duty or responsibility to yourself to play. I say to myself, there are traders in pain here, losing their cars and houses, whatever, and it's time to play. I have to take action. You can smell the blood of other people's losses. That has to kick up on your radar screen, you must seize that advantage. In fact, that's what makes the game worth playing!
>
> I actively search for opportunities that no one else is looking for. And I have the confidence to do the trades, to try them

and to know that I'll be wrong a lot. And I have the conviction that overall I'm still going to come out way ahead.

What happens to me a lot of times is I do a great deal of
work on a theory or strategy and the actual trade comes down
to no value. And unless you derive that pure joy of identifying
and getting the edge when it is there for a minute, a day, a
week, or a month, then you won't be able to tolerate all the
dead ends. As long as that joy is with me I've got to be confident that I'm going to stay at the head of the pack. I know
and have seen fertile areas of opportunity come and go because information has become more widely accessible. My
edge is to constantly stay out in front of the curve. I'm not
afraid to identify it and then take my shot!

Conviction

When it comes to operating in the stock market, the trader
must develop a system of personal beliefs about oneself and the
market that fosters excellence. Angelo Reynolds, a professional market maker, puts it this way:

> I learned a long time ago in sports that there is a world of dif-
> ference between thinking and doing. I was afraid at first and
> I think it was a very natural fear. I mean I was going against
> some of the best traders in the world. But in no way did I ever
> believe that I wasn't going to succeed like I have in everything
> else I have done in my life.

Or consider this comment from Marshall Stein, a former market maker who now trades his own account:

> Trading has certainly taught me about my personal strengths
> and weaknesses. It has taught me how I react under situations
> of stress. Trading has allowed me to have a measure of cour-

age in what I do for a living. It has shown me that I have the capability to rise to an occasion to exhibit, if you will, grace under fire.

It's not like I go around pounding my chest, but it's a comforting thought to know that I have the courage to trade markets at times when it feels like I should run scared. I can exercise strength of character to either stick with it or get out. It's the analysis sometimes, or the work that you've done. It's the culmination of your thinking that you've put into action. I think what distinguishes me from most is that I have really done just about everything that is possible in my profession and I am still on the lookout for new challenges.

Constructing New Patterns of Behavior

The online trader who has difficulty executing trades must interrupt old patterns of behavior and substitute them with new ones. If you have difficulty taking losses in the market, or buying at predefined opportunity points when everyone else is selling, or catching breakouts, or has too big of an ego when it comes to trading, you know you must make changes to secure a more profitable result! Top traders have developed techniques for constructing new patterns of behavior that empower them to act decisively and automatically in the stock market. Robin Mesch, a trader and former chief fixed income technical analyst for Thomson Research—one of the largest providers of proprietary financial services in the world—put it this way:

> There's a phase that you go through where you think you can't lose. And you believe you know exactly what the market is going to do next. Then to compound problems, you think *since I can't lose I might as well pyramid as the market is going against me.* That's how strong you feel about that. But you need those experiences of being wrong so you can learn to become a disciplined trader, which in the final analysis is ulti-

51

mate control. You learn from your mistakes if you're committed to paying attention.

Arlene Busch heads a highly successful group of proprietary equities traders. When she hires new traders she's most wary of a trader's ego.

> One of the things that I pride myself on is not having an ego about this business. Having a big ego about trading is a recipe for disaster. It's what will make a trader lose every penny he's made. If I find a trader in the group who has a big ego, I immediately let him go. I don't care how much money he's making. You can tell by watching how he's trading. He'll get stubborn about a position. He'll think that he's right and the market is wrong! The market is never wrong; the market is always right!
>
> But you can see his ego in other things as well. You see it in his habits and possessions. He drives a Ferrari. He wears a gold Rolex! He lives in an outlandish house. He flies the Concorde. I don't want traders who do this. I want traders who respect the market and keep their personal egos in check.

Conditioning

Finally, once you have developed a new pattern of behavior, substituting winning techniques and strategies for losing ones, it is critical to reinforce those positive behaviors in order to condition yourself to act automatically and unemotionally in the market. You must discipline yourself, condition your nervous system to react with clinical and methodical deliberation at points of opportunity. Discipline does and will produce confidence and ultimate success.

One top trader expressed this same idea this way:

> All successful trading comes down to three things, knowledge, nerve, and the ability to take a loss. Everybody has the ability

to lose money! But it takes nerve to lose and then come right back, to have the audacity to assume that you're smart enough to make your trade, take advantage of an opportunity, and make money. I found that the psychology of being able to lose money and come back was a key factor for me. It's very easy to have a drawdown and become discouraged. You have to have a great deal of confidence in yourself that even though you've taken a beating in the market, you can return and trade effectively.

Establishing trading goals not only identifies exactly what the online trader needs to accomplish to enhance market performance, it also serves as motivation. There has been ample research that demonstrates the importance of a clearly defined goal as a compelling source of positive personal motivation.

When I conduct workshops with traders, I always ask them the following seven questions. Write down your answers, a simple yes or no will suffice.

1. Do you have a clearly defined set of trading goals, in writing?
2. Do you have an explicit description of performance, outcome, and motivational goals for the next month, year, and three years?
3. Are you doing something every day to move you closer to your short-term trading goal?
4. Are you doing something today to move you closer to your long-term trading goals?
5. Do you have a clear idea of what you are trying to accomplish in the market, based on your approach, system, or strategy?
6. Do you focus more on procedures than goals when it comes to your trading or investment decisions?
7. Do you evaluate your progress as a trader more on accomplishment than activity?

As you review your answers, I'm sure you will see how they provide valuable information for you to improve.

THE IMPORTANCE OF TRADING GOALS

Goal	Benefit	Trading Behavior
Performance goal	Focuses on improvement in relation to your own standards.	Increases physical and psychological skills related to trading.
Outcome goal	Helps determine what's important to you.	Allows for the development of techniques and strategies that match your personality.
Motivation	Helps increase effort and direct attention.	Allows traders to maintain a high level of enthusiasm and confidence.

CRITERIA FOR TRADING GOALS

The criteria for establishing a trading goal should satisfy the basic requirements of any goal.

- *Specific.* Goal is clear, precise, well defined.
- *Time-framed.* Goal states a specific period.
- *Positive.* Goal is stated in a way that is empowering.
- *Control.* Goal should be completely within your control.
- *Realistic.* Your goal is attainable under market constraints in place during your time frame.
- *Measurable.* Goal should be easily quantifiable.

As you think about your own online trading goals, answer the following five questions. Be as specific as you can. The more you put into this exercise, the greater the return. Research has shown that writing down your goals greatly increases your commitment and the ultimate likelihood of achieving your goals.

1. What are your trading goals (performance, outcome, motivation)?
2. What do you want to accomplish in the short term? In the long term?
3. Why is it important for you to achieve your trading goals?
4. What is preventing you from achieving your trading goals now? Be honest with yourself!
5. What specific steps can you take to achieve goals? Be specific!

Now that you have answered these questions and have a better understanding of your personal goals, let's take a look at the recorded goals of other traders.

The following is a list of goals from traders I have worked with on an individual basis and from participants in my trading seminars. As you consider these goals, be reminded that individuals were asked to have these goals satisfy all the criteria of goal setting that we discussed earlier. In other words, operational definitions were required when individuals stated abstract ideas. Goals included:

- To have more control over my emotions when I trade
- To have more confidence when taking losses
- To be consistently profitable
- To develop a trading system that is consistent with my personality and to readily apply it
- To define my losses and not dwell on them
- To consistently be aware that investing and trading is a process and not just a series of independent trades
- To have a high level of self-esteem when I trade
- To be a disciplined trader

- To focus on opportunities
- To catch breakouts when trading momentum
- To take all my signals
- To have control over my trades
- To establish limited risk and limitless profit potential
- To become a better investor by constantly trying to learn more about myself
- To operate completely in the here and now

MONTHLY GOAL CHART

In order to meet personal goals, each trader must set specific smaller goals that will lead to attaining overall goals. Determine what steps you must take.

- My long-term goal
- My goal for this month
- My goal for this week
- My strategy for achieving this goal
- Anxieties or impediments I need to overcome to achieve my goal

OVERCOMING IMPEDIMENTS

As you think about what you have written, I would like you to be aware of those factors or personal anxieties that you identified as impediments to achieving your goals.

I believe, based on my experience and interviews, that the factors which have prevented most traders from achieving their trading goals fall into five broad categories. They are:

1. Self-limiting beliefs
2. Unresourceful state

3. Poor focus
4. Ill-defined personal strategy
5. Lack of physical and psychological energy

Self-Limiting Beliefs

Self-limiting beliefs are inhibiting beliefs that traders possess about themselves and/or the market. Examples of such beliefs are:

- I don't have enough conviction.
- I'm never quite sure I know what I'm doing.
- How can I be sure?
- I can't trust my judgment.
- I don't believe in myself.
- It's impossible to make money in these volatile markets.

Unresouceful State

An unresourceful state is when a trader is in a state of mind that is guided by fear, anxiety, and confusion. Traders reported the following.

- I'm really angry.
- This is frustrating.
- I'm too stupid.
- I'm afraid.
- I'm too small a player.

Poor Focus

Poor focus is when trades are made as a result of distracted attention. You didn't zero in on the essentials. Traders have said:

- Those bad fills always get in my way.
- I'm always thinking about something else at just the wrong time.
- I'm so distracted by procedures I don't have the ability to look at what's really important.
- I can't see the big picture.

Ill-Defined Personal Strategy

An ill-defined personal strategy is characterized by trades that are made by the seat of one's pants. In this condition, trading is an immediate response to emotion. Traders who have experienced this report:

- I don't have a clear plan.
- I never know when to take profits.
- My methodology lacks consistency.
- Sometimes it works and sometimes it doesn't.
- How do you know when to get out of a market?

Lack of Physical and Psychological Energy

Lack of physical and psychological energy occurs when one's anxiety level produces tension which results in physical and psychological fatigue. Traders have told me:

- This market totally wipes me out.
- I just don't have enough energy.
- The market action just drives me nuts.

THE EDGE THAT MAKES
THE DIFFERENCE

Professional traders, especially the successful ones, always speak of "getting the edge." Their edge is the overriding ability to be resilient to whatever the market sends in their direction and knowing what to do next with little emotional impact: being able to maintain unassailable confidence in themselves and their approach at all times. However, without exception, the top traders understand that their edge has little to do with the commonsense or conventional notion of getting a good fill in the market.

For the top traders, investing is at its roots a process and although methodologies vary widely, all share a common unquenchable desire to become successful. Other commonalties in capturing the edge included:

- A personal discipline based on research, independence, and patience
- A love of trading
- Well-defined risk management
- Total acceptance of losing as part of the trading process

The edge that makes the difference, then, comes down to this:

- *Fully understand your motives for trading.* Once you know what your motives are, examine them carefully. Most traders trade in a constant state of conflict. My experience reveals that many people who think they want to trade really don't.
- *Develop a personal strategy that works for you and fits your personality.* If the system you're using doesn't feel right, you're going to lose before you even start.
- *It has to be fun.* I can't stress this point enough. Trading has to literally feel good. You must be in a frame of mind that allows you to enjoy the process effortlessly, be resourceful

FIGURE 4.1   Critical Factors in Having the Edge

Trader Response	Having the Edge	Losing the Edge
Patience	Waits for opportunities to materialize based on well-thought-out game plan.	Plans very little; reacts according to personal whim.
Discipline	Sees the big picture; responds deliberately.	Is emotional, anxious and often confused about what to do.
Strategy	Plans carefully; limits losses; lets profits run.	Plans little or not at all; does not rely on consistent methodology.
Expertise	Is well-prepared; has done the necessary homework.	Knows little about market; is unprepared.
Motive	Has long-term motive, e.g., intellectual challenge.	Wants to make money; wants instant gratification.
Goals	Defines goals clearly.	Has ill-defined goals.
Risk control	Wants highly controlled risk/reward ratio.	Has little or no control over risk/reward ratio.
State of mind	Has positive, resourceful, empowering beliefs and focus. Has high level of self-esteem and trust; is relaxed and confident.	Is nervous, anxious; believes the worst will happen. Focus is distracted; trades in conflict.

and make good judgments—even when you are losing! You don't have to like losing, but you do have to have a sense of equilibrium.

- *Hard work is essential.* There's no way to get around it. You must put in the time. As Thomas Edison said, "A lot of people do not recognize opportunity because it usually goes around wearing overalls, looking like hard work."

- *Confidence.* You must possess a repertoire of personal beliefs that constantly reinforces feelings of high self-esteem and confidence in your analysis and execution of trades, whether you win or lose. Discipline, patience, personal responsibility, and repeated success make this a lot easier.
- *Positive state of mind.* All top-performing traders have developed an internal mental terrain that reduces anxiety and promotes excellence. They manage to achieve this end by internally representing external events in such a way that assures success, adjusting and redefining as they deem appropriate. They do this by employing a belief system that does not allow for the concept of failure and a personal focus that concentrates on what is essential to achieving this end. In short, they have mastered the ability to create states of mind and body that are resourceful and that assure whatever it takes to succeed.

If you are at a point now where you are saying to yourself "hey, this stuff is obvious!" you are not missing the point: it is simple but not easily accomplished. My grandfather used to have an expression, "easy to read, hard to achieve," that about sums up top flight trading! What is important for the trader to know is that subtleties of thought and action produce results. Recognizing the power of the online trader's beliefs about the market and self as well as how one directs his or her focus is essential.

Belief

Belief is the window through which we see the world and through which we are ourselves. Whatever you do in life will be affected by what you believe in—what you believe about yourself and others. Your actions are a direct result of the quality and intensity of your beliefs. What you believe about yourself as a trader will determine not only the results of your trading decisions but also how you experience the entire trading process. In the E*Trade commercial this point is made very compellingly: Stuart's experience online is quite different from everyone else's! He is totally absorbed, confident—sure of himself, his strategy, and his inevitable success.

Our beliefs are deeply felt certainties that we possess about ourselves and the world we live in. What we believe determines what we focus on; what meaning we assign to what we see and what actions result. This process of belief/focus/action not only determines our success as online traders but in a very real sense, our success as human beings. See how belief and focus impact our ability to make sound trading decisions.

Positive trading → Focus → Trading decision
Belief system   (Dictated by belief)   (Directed by focus)

The Power of Belief and Focus in Making Sound Online Trading Decisions

Online Trading Belief →	Focus →	Trading Decision
I'm a disciplined trader. I can make money by capitalizing on stock market opportunities.	I buy only when I determine there is value and market opportunity according to a specific game plan with defined loss.	I confidently take a profit or loss based on a well planned and calculated methodology.

The following comment is what Jack Sandner said about the importance of belief and focus in trading:

> I think you'd have to go back to the recesses of the mind, what makes someone competitive, and what makes someone want to win. You learn that the desire to win and the ability to try to figure a way to win in whatever venue you're involved com-

plement one another. For example, if it's boxing, the desire to win may translate into training very, very hard, working on different skill sets rather than just going in and being a brawler. You'll find a way to win, and usually it's through hard work and discipline. . . .

In boxing, if you're fighting a certain kind of a fighter, you'll fight a little differently. Is he a strong puncher or a stick-and-move-type of fighter? I'm always trying to find a way to score the points to win or to get the knockout. But the main thing is to walk out the winner at the end! I think everybody prepares for trading differently. In my case, I think because of my competitive nature, I saw the markets as just another event. . . .

I think I just always had the intuitive feeling that winning was a protracted experience in trading and not a one-time thing. Once you can adjust to that and truly understand it's the whole game that counts, then you can look at the market in an objective way.

It isn't a daily thing, because nobody can be a daily winner. You develop rules and discipline and an approach. Of course, you also have to know that to win you must create a set of standards and movements. And it takes time to do that through trial and error! But the key is to respond as a winner to what happens to you in the market. If the fear of losing is so extraordinary that it inhibits you from moving forward, you cannot be a trader. Also you cannot be an all-or-nothing trader. You can't trade with the attitude that I'm going to make a million today or I'm going to lose everything I have. That's a disaster! I say you must view trading as a protracted experience and then know how you respond as an individual. I find that people who turn out to be terrible traders are the ones who don't know how to respond to what they would define as a loss. They just don't know how to react. Their fear of losing keeps them in the market too long! It puts them in positions that they wouldn't otherwise have been in. Ultimately you need to have a healthy respect for the market, and the fear of losing cannot be so pervasive in your system that it doesn't allow you to trade to win. You can watch children as they are growing up. You can tell which kid plays not to lose and which one plays all-out to win. There's also the kid who won't dive off the board because he's just too afraid! Or the opposite, the kid who is reckless and gets hurt. To be a successful trader, you need to understand the balance point between being too afraid and too aggressive.

Howard Abell (*Digital Day Trading*, 1998) offered this opinion:

Traders have to understand exactly how they are reacting both physically and mentally to the stock market. They have to understand their own feelings and the emotional process that is taking place when they're taking losses or profits or deciding, sometimes in anguish, whether or not to take a trade.

Traders need to look at what makes their successes successful—and very objectively attempt to make themselves operate in the successful mode all the time or as much of the time as possible. It requires a great deal of introspection and looking at yourself and the trading process under a microscope. Trading is self-discovery. You can tell who you are and what you are by how you trade.

The reward of all this self-analysis is the ability to cultivate what we call trading intuition. Without the work—without the commitment to put in the time and look at how you are internalizing market events—there will be no strong and reliable feel for the market or intuition in the end.

Peter Mulmat, a successful S&P 500 trader had this to say:

To be successful, you have to constantly be willing to reevaluate what you're doing and be innovative in your trading ideas. I think the most successful traders are always retooling their market theories. They are always readjusting their strategies to current conditions and perceptions. I think everyone else is kind of one step behind. You need to be able to first identify what's absolutely relevant right now. It may be different tomorrow. The worst thing you can do is become complacent. You have to be able to challenge yourself. There are always ways to improve on what you're doing and the methodology by which you do it.

This does not only mean looking at new markets to trade and looking at new ways to trade. It may mean just trading during the day or taking advantage of options to hedge positions. I think you have to be willing to innovate and to constantly be committed to look ahead. Of course, the worst thing to do is to grasp onto what people are doing right now and feel that this will make you successful. You must learn to identify opportunity and trust yourself.

Be prepared to work very hard. Be prepared to arm yourself with the educational quantitative tools you need to be able to succeed at trading. Remember the people you're competing against. And it is a competition! You're going against the very best! Like any other competition—be it athletic or scholastic—you won't place at the top unless you're willing to fully prepare yourself.

5

Developing Confidence

Confidence is the trader's ultimate bet on one's own ability. It is the dominant message in the Ameritrade commercial which counsels "Believe in Yourself."

The stock market opens and your 1000 share position of Dell is two points against you and you know exactly what to do next! Or it is two points in your favor and based on your risk parameters you know exactly the next right step to take in the market, as it is happening, based on a well-defined and executed plan.

Possessing confidence allows the trader not to get caught up in the fury and excitement of market activity. It allows the trader in varying scenarios to stay focused and maintain discipline to do the "right thing" given an external tide of reports, analyses, and opinions; and an internal psychology that explains and excuses based on feelings of fear and greed.

Confidence is expecting the best of yourself and believing in a positive outcome for your trading decisions. This is not wishful thinking or new age positivism! It is quite literally believing in an optimistic outcome based on your research and discipline. This form of thinking allows you to maximize profits and not get out of the market too soon—at the first sign of a reversal—as long as the move is consistent with your overall approach. Conversely, it does allow you to get out soon enough when the market violates your stop loss so that you do not find yourself in a position where you are playing "catch up," hoping the market will come back your way.

One of the most difficult lessons a trader has to learn is how to take a loss. There is much truth to the old trading axiom "your first loss is your best loss." However, as I mentioned earlier, it is one thing to know an axiom, quite another to apply it flawlessly.

Fear is the opposite of confidence. It is a negative market expectation and it is what prevents a trader from taking a loss or executing ("pulling the trigger") at the point of market opportunity. The interesting thing to note here is that both confidence and fear are based on expectation of what is to come, before it actually happens. The trader who can't make the trade consciously or unconsciously fears the future loss!

This intense feeling of fear (market paralysis), is well presented in an E*Trade commercial. There is a trader who realizes a market opportunity but cannot bring himself to click his mouse. He jogs around his room, exercises vigorously, and seeks other distractions until he can finally bring himself to a point of ultimate relief; clicking the mouse and making the trade!

Think of the many times in your life when you approached a difficult challenge, burdened with a consuming feeling of fear. Remember how your expectation affected what you were feeling. Consider how it directed your focus or motivated your plan of action. Now, remember a time when you approached a difficult challenge bolstered with a feeling of complete confidence. Remember how your expectation affected what you were feeling then. Consider how that strong positive outlook directed your focus and motivated your plan of action. I think by now you will readily see the importance of confidence for a successful market result.

Tim McAuliffe is a professional market maker who appeared with me on a CNBC program that highlighted the winning psychology of professional traders. A former athlete, Mr. McAuliffe made the following comment:

With three seconds left in a basketball game I want the ball. I'm not going to pass off, hesitate, or throw up a brick. It's not that I'm hogging the ball or arrogant; I just believe that in the clutch I can get the job done!

Jack Sandner had this to say:

You have to have a tremendous confidence in yourself and your ability, and that trading is a cycle like everything else, and at the end of the term it will turn your way if you believe in yourself and do all the right things.

Tom Grossman, who manages a $500 million equities fund said:

When I'm playing golf, if there is a gun pointed to my head, I'm still focused on the shot (no pun intended). And I'm going to make it. And, in fact, I have no right to think of myself as a great putter. Clearly, if it could be measured quantitatively, there are much better putters in the world. But if you put a gun to my head and said make this ten-footer straight up a hill, in my mind no one is going to do a better job than me. Not Tiger Woods or anyone else. Thank you very much, I'll do it myself!

It is important to recognize that although these comments may sound arrogant and egotistical, they are, in fact, a psychological expression of fully prepared and focused minds who believe no matter what the market sends their way, they will be able to operate effectively. This does not mean each of their investment decisions will result in a profitable outcome. However, it reveals the confidence that they experience knowing the next right step to take in the market.

POSITIVE EXPECTATIONS

Positive expectation → Sound market → Positive trading
(confidence)   strategy (based   result (whether or
                          on a plan)   not individual trade
                                             was profitable)

NEGATIVE EXPECTATIONS

Negative expectation → Unsound market → Negative market
(fear, uncertainty,   strategy (based   result (whether or
inability to pull the   on emotion)   not individual
trigger)   trade is profitable)

THE SYNTAX OF
SUCCESSFUL TRADING

A self-confident trader can effect trades that will more often result in success. The steps of a successful trade—whether or not it results in a gain, are:

Well analyzed trade
  ↓
System of empowering personal beliefs and attitudes
  ↓
Proper execution based on positive focus
  ↓
Decisive, resourceful state of mind
  ↓
Successful trading performance

Confidence based on competence, as we have seen, is a result of motivation, belief in oneself and the market, and the trader's state of mind. Again, in psychological terms, it is no more than consistently expecting a positive outcome based on trading a sound investment plan.

In *Reminiscences of a Stock Operator* (Wiley, 1994), Edwin Lefevre writes, "It takes a man a long time to learn all the lessons of all his mistakes. They say that there are two sides to everything. But there is only one side to the stock market; and it is not the bull side or the bear side, but the right side. It took longer to get that general principle fixed firmly in my mind than it did most of the more technical phases of the game of speculation." To be on the "right" side of the market takes confidence; the ability to take profit when it is there and manage losses that are the inevitable, not accidental, opposites of risk.

Let's focus now on the issue of trading losses. In my experience most investment and trading books either ignore the subject entirely or write about it in passing, as if loss is not an inevitable element of the trading process. Being a mentally tough online trader requires fully understanding the issue of loss so that it doesn't detract from your overall market behavior.

In *The Psychology of Technical Analysis* (McGraw-Hill, 1994), Tony Plummer very succinctly stated the problem: "The question for the trader is whether it is really possible to divorce the longer-term goal of profitable trading from the potentially traumatic short-term affects of incurring losses." In my experience most traders deal with the issue of loss in a variety of maladaptive ways, the most common of which are:

- Denial
- Inaction
- Confusion
- Anger

Denial

Is it any wonder that many traders are not getting the results they want in the market? I think not! The reason I have come to this conclusion is that most traders choose to trade with their eyes closed, ears shut, and nervous system turned off. How else could you tolerate a trade that continues going against you, day after day, with no defined risk, until the discomfort has gotten so severe that nothing can stave off the pain? Denial won't help!

Inaction

There is an old folk saying: "If you sleep on the floor you can't fall out of bed." Many traders have adopted this "position" when it comes to the question of risk. If you don't pull the trigger, they think, you can't miss the target. But the truth of the matter is you have to pick up the gun and steady your aim—that is, know what you're shooting at—so you can pull the trigger with confidence. Developing a strategy with a specific point of focus and possessing the intellectual recognition that taking a loss (the real fear) is not only inevitable, but essential, will give you the conviction to exploit market opportunities.

It is only when missing out becomes more psychologically painful than being inactive that triggers get pulled and targets get hit.

Confusion

Confusion and uncertainty result from not working out a well-defined risk management formula prior to opening the specific trade that you're in. You will recognize that reevaluating the cost of your summer vacation at the time your Coca-Cola position is sinking to new lows is not an optimal trading strategy. The more emotion you eliminate from your trading, the greater your sense of clarity about market decisions. Jeffery Silverman made this point very well when he said, "Doing things that avoid having an emotional content in your decision-making is where all the discipline comes in. Be unemotional about getting in, be unemotional about the position, and be unemotional when getting out."

Anger

Reacting to the market out of anger is like choosing to hold your breath until your neighbor turns blue. It's not going to work! Your anger will not undo a loss. It certainly may influence it negatively by leading you to actions that turn a small loss into a large loss!

SYMPTOMS OF TAKING A LOSS

The wrong psychological and emotional responses can inhibit the development and implementation of an effective trading strategy. Learning to take a loss is the single hardest lesson a trader has to learn. This is no intellectual exercise. Taking a loss involves every aspect of the human being, as illustrated below.

Physical symptoms:

- Rapid or shallow breathing
- Sweating
- Constriction of muscles
- Upset stomach
- Tension
- Feeling of malaise

Emotional symptoms:

- Anger
- Depression

- Disillusionment
- Distraction
- Generalized anxiety
- Irritability
- Frustration
- Low self-worth
- Embarrassment

Visual imagery traders process internally:

- Images of past failures
- Pictures of trading obstacles and disappointments
- Visions of unrelated mishaps of a generalized nature

Auditory imagery traders process internally:

- The voice of doom and failure
- Replaying negative experiences from the past
- Remembering why you are such a "jerk"

Kinesthetic (sensory) imagery traders experience:

- Body feels heavy
- Shoulders droop
- Torso is hunched
- Facial muscles slacken
- Breathing is short and shallow
- Eyes are cast down
- Trader feels slow, weak, or out of energy

Anxiety traders experience:

- Fear of failure. Trader feels intense pressure to perform and ties self-worth to trading.
- Fear of success. Trader loses control: euphoric trading; trader doubts himself or herself.

- Fear of inadequacy. Trader experiences loss of self-esteem and diminished confidence.
- Loss of control. Trader loses sense of personal responsibility when trading; feels market is out to get him or her.

Thoughts traders have:

- I don't know what I'm doing.
- These markets are impossible.
- I'm too small, inexperienced, young, old, etc.
- I don't have a clear strategy.
- What will [someone] think of me?
- I'm a loser, fool, idiot, etc.

Beliefs traders have about the market:

- The market is rigged.
- It's impossible to have a winning trade.
- The market makers always pick me off.
- You can never get a decent fill.

Beliefs traders have about themselves:

- I can never make a winning trade.
- I'm such a _____ I can never make a good trade.
- I have to be perfect.
- If I take a loss, then I'm a loser.
- If the market doesn't do exactly what I expect, I don't know anything.

Self-defeating attitudes traders possess:

- Holding oneself to impossible standards
- Trying to please others
- Thinking in absolute terms (black or white, all or nothing, total success or failure)

- Focusing on negative things
- Believing your childhood or past experiences have pro-grammed you for failure
- Demanding certainty of yourself and the market
- Defining trading as impossible
- Representing a bad trade as a catastrophe
- Labeling yourself in a globally negative way rather than just looking at the trade.

In a cover article in *The New York Times Magazine* titled, *Riding the Mo in the Lime Green Glow*, a successful online trader casually explains his approach.

> In one of the books I read, the author compares a trader to a ninja—the way they hide out, they're in black and they can sit there and you can't even hear them breathe. They wait for the perfect moment and then they strike. It's like you could go a whole week and not trade at all until you find the perfect stock.

The Trading Syntax of the Successful Trader

Top traders believe that successful trading has its own arrangement of internal representations and proven market behaviors that are executed in a specific sequence of actions to achieve a profitable result. In contrast, the negative way most traders internally represent market phenomena dictates a response of indecision, anxiety, or confusion and produces a result which they find unsatisfying. The important point here is that profitable traders are successful because their actions are true to a specific syntax which ideally looks like:

Well analyzed $\rightarrow$ Proper $\rightarrow$ Decisive, resourceful $\rightarrow$ Profitable
trade execution state of mind trade

Bernard Baruch had a simple recipe for success: "Take the obvious, add a cupful of brains, a generous pinch of imagination, a bucketful of courage and daring, stir well, and bring to a boil." Being a mentally tough trader requires no less. The simple (though not easy to achieve) recipe for traders is:

- Identify market signal
- React automatically with confidence
- Feel good (confident, high self-esteem, etc.) about the trade

IDENTIFY MARKET SIGNAL

This is your point of opportunity. It can be a point, line, number, or value area that you have predetermined and analyzed as a viable market entry.

React Automatically

This is where the "rubber meets the road." Here is where you react decisively, taking action at your opportunity with confidence and a positive state of mind.

FEEL GOOD ABOUT THE TRADE

Your decision is based on methodology and discipline, not emotion. You must feel good about the trade whether any single investment decision is profitable or not.

Most traders' recipes look more like this:

- Identify market signal
- React with confusion, anxiety, or inconsistency
- Feel "bad" (angry, nervous, hesitant) about the trade

As we review all the psychological skills already mentioned, we must ask ourselves two basic questions: (1) What are the market behaviors that prevent most traders from achieving the results they desire? (2) What psychological factors inhibit most traders from applying specific skills when trading?

In my experience and in the view of the top traders I have interviewed, there are essential psychological barriers to successful trading.

Not defining a loss. No one enters an online trade assuming it will result in a loss. No one buys a stock expecting the market has topped out. Conversely, no one sells short expecting the market will rally to new highs. However, this occurs all too often. So upon entering any trade, it is important that you already have your risk defined! If you are afraid to take a loss, don't trade.

Not taking a loss or a profit. There is an old trading axiom "your first loss is the best loss." It's true. Losing is an integral part of the process. So is the opposite, taking profits. If the market has reached your objective, don't be afraid to take your profit. Many times the market will not give you a second chance.

Getting locked into a belief. Don't put yourself in prison. As George Segal succinctly put it, "The market is the boss." Your belief that AOL is going to the moon or that Yahoo! is going to hell in a handbasket is irrelevant. The market tells you everything! Listen! Remember what Yogi Berra said, "You can observe a lot by just watching."

Getting "Boston strangled." There is an old Henny Youngman joke that was popular in the early 1960s at the time the Boston Strangler (a serial killer) was not yet in police custody. A man is sitting in his living room, reading the evening newspaper and he hears a knock at the front door. Walking up to the door but not opening it he asks, "Who is it?"

78

The psychopath answers, "It's the Boston Strangler."

The man walks back into the apartment, passes the living room and into the kitchen, turns to his wife and says, "It's for you, dear!"

I always relate this anecdote at trading seminars as an analogy to taking a trade from someone else that you have no control over. In other words, a tip is like getting "Boston strangled." Don't do it! This is one door you don't want to open!

Kamikaze trading. Don't trade like you're a kamikaze pilot. Don't let external pressure make you stray from your system. You'll crash land.

Euphoric trading. The opposite of kamikaze trading. You're feeling absolutely invincible. Heroic. Untouchable. Now, get back to your system.

Hesitating at your numbers. You've worked on your daily, weekly, and monthly charts. You've studied Gann, Fibonnaci, Wycoff, and Elliott Wave. The market comes right down to your number, line, area, but you hesitate and don't buy.

Not catching a breakout. It's like going to the airport and watching the planes take off. Wouldn't it be fun to be on board and arrive at a profitable destination!

Not focusing on opportunities. There are so many distractions in the market. How do you keep your focus clear and laser-straight? How do you get beyond all the false opportunities?

Being more invested in being right than in making money. In almost every trading room throughout the world there are people who run around announcing to their colleagues that they have the high/low of every move. What they don't possess are profits. The name of the game is making money.

Not consistently applying your trading system. If it's any good, you have to use it consistently. As the saying goes, "if you don't use it. . . . lose it."

Not having a well-defined money management program. You have heard this one many times before, "But the trade looked so good, so right." The object of money management is preservation of capital.

Not being in the right state of mind. In my experience, more than 80 percent of all trading failure is the result of not being in the right state of mind. The right state of mind produces the right results. As Gene Agatstein observed, "You get exactly the results you want. You produce your own success."

SUMMARY

Successful trading, then, comes down to this: overcome your personal psychological barriers and condition yourself to produce feelings of self-trust, high self-esteem, unshakable conviction, and confidence. These steps will lead to good judgment and winning trades based on a proven methodology.

6

Controlling Anxiety

The daily market's conflicting and contradictory information easily provokes an investor's feelings of anxiety. To be able to exploit opportunity successfully the trader must learn to manage anxiety to minimize its debilitating effects on one's performance. A well-planned strategy minimizes anxiety by addressing those factors (e.g., loss, risk-control, market re-entry) that inevitably produce inhibiting feelings. Figure 6.1 illustrates sources of trading anxiety.

The key to minimizing feelings of anxiety is understanding and then implementing a well-tested stock market strategy that has a proven methodology. It is important to note here the difference between market strategy and tactics. A strategy is a process of determining your major trading goals and then adopting a course of action whereby you allocate the resources necessary to achieve those goals. Tactics are a means of translating broad strategic goals into specific investment objectives that are relevant to a single component of your trading plan. In order for a trading strategy to be successful, it must incorporate all the psychological, technical, and financial resources that are at your disposal. In metaphorical terms, your strategy is the bull's-eye; specific trading tactics are the arrows

FIGURE 6.1 Sources of Trading Anxiety and Solutions

Anxiety	Manifestation	Solution
Fear of failure	Trader feels intense pressure to perform, ties self-worth to trading, becomes a perfectionist, or is overly concerned about what others think.	Focus on applying your methodology and mentally rehearse the mechanics of the trade. Also rehearse the attitude in your mind that trading is not about proving anything to anybody. The closer you can get to focusing on your methodology, the more you will feel in control of this anxiety.
Fear of success	Trader loses control or engages in "euphoric" trading. Trader doubts himself or herself.	If your trading approach has shown statistical reliability in its performance, rehearse feelings of confidence as you mentally run through the placement, management, and closing out of the trade. Feel in a literal sense how you personally experience confidence.
Loss of control	Trader feels market is out to get him or her. (It's not!) Trader loses sense of personal responsibility when trading.	Teach yourself how to get into a physically and psychologically relaxed state when trading. Focus on your specific methodology and expect small losses!

that allow you to hit the target of your overall trading goals. The difficulty with most trading strategies is that they don't adequately deal with the central issues of trading; namely the psychological factors that produce anxiety and degrade the trader's state of mind.

STRATEGY

The trader must understand what I believe to be the essential elements of a successful trading strategy. Once one understands these elements, one can recognize personal strengths and weaknesses and make trading goals that accommodate those realities.

You Assume Personal Responsibility
for All Market Actions

You produce the results. No matter whom you listen to, what reports you read, what analyses you consult, you choose the trading strategy and you are responsible for the results. Good or bad, the buck stops with you! The Nordstrom Corporation Policy Manual has just one sentence in it. "Use your own best judgment at all times."

You Must Take into Consideration
Your Motive for Trading

Your trading strategy must reflect your motive for trading. J. P. Morgan said, "A person usually has two reasons for doing something: a good reason and the real reason."

You Trade to Win

Most traders don't trade to win; they trade not to lose. To win you have to risk loss. An effective strategy adopts a proactive market behavior that allows you to play full out. You strategize to buy aggressively at your numbers, catch breakouts, and enter and exit the market at your signals.

You Establish Goals and Formulate a Plan to Take Action

Your strategy builds in long-range and short-range goals. What is it you are tying to accomplish today? This week? This month? This year? What specific plan for outcome, performance, and motivation can you adopt right now to achieve these goals?

You Control Anxiety

As you have read and perhaps experienced, there are many anxieties attached to trading. A well-planned strategy addresses those factors (e.g., loss, risk-control, market re-entry) that produce anxiety. The fear of making a mistake can be much more debilitating than almost any mistake you can make.

You Create a Point of Focus

The problem with most trading strategies is that in the final analysis they lack a point of focus. To be successful, you must know what you're looking for and what you're looking at. You must be able to distinguish the signal from the noise, winning from losing trades, high probability from low probability outcomes.

You Choose a Strategy That Is Consistent and Congruent with Your Personality

Many traders complain that their strategy just doesn't "feel right," "look right," or "sound right." For your strategy to be successful it must fit you. If it doesn't, it will produce anxiety.

You Have an Edge

Unfortunately there is no "edge" sold at the local department store, ready-made, one-size-fits-all. Your edge is your personality, information, knowledge of your strengths and weaknesses, and your own trading style. You must find your own edge to having a winning strategy!

Your Strategy Is Automatic, Effortless, and Decisive

"He who hesitates is lost." The trader must be able to respond to market conditions, unimpaired by internal or external hindrances.

You Manage Risk and Assume Losses

A good trading strategy has the inevitability of loss built into it so that when you lose, it is not seen as unusual. Risk management assumes that no single loss will ever get out of hand. As in baseball, hitting safely three out of ten times can pay off very handsomely. Your strategy must inform you with certainty when it needs to be returned to current long-term conditions.

You Allow for Patience and Trade in a Resourceful State of Mind

Once the trade is made, your strategy must allow you to remain calm, patient, and focused. Your strategy must have contingency plans for dealing with a variety of market scenarios. Anything less is gambling!

If you bet on a horse, that's gambling; if you bet you can pull three spades, that's entertainment. If you bet cotton will go up three cents, that's business. See the difference?—William F. Sherrod

You Are Profit Oriented, Practical Rather Than Theoretical

This point may seem obvious but its implementation is often lost. Many traders develop stock market strategies consistent with a particular ideological or technical bias rather than with making money. The name of the game is performance (read *money*)!

Winston Churchill said, "It is a socialist idea that making profits is a vice; I consider the real vice is making losses." This is just as true in trading.

You Leave No Uncertainty

Think in probabilities, trade in certainties. Your strategy tells you when to act decisively.

Your Strategy Allows You to Produce Consistent Results

Your strategy provides the organization and order to allow you to be consistent. The rest is up to you! Remember, positive consistency based on research and testing is the desired result.

You Identify Opportunities

According to Anthony Robbins,

> The difference between those who succeed and those who fail isn't what they have—it's what they choose to see and do with their resources and their experiences of life.

This also applies to trading. Your trading strategy should allow you to open your eyes and see market opportunities so that you can act!

THE INNER AND OUTER GAMES OF TRADING

As we have seen, there is an inner and outer division to investing and trading. Being a mentally tough online trader involves mastering those strategies—internal and external—that assure excellent investment results. The *internal dimension* focuses on those issues that influence the way we internalize market phenomena; that is, the way we personally represent the market (e.g., profits, losses, price action, etc.) to ourselves. The *external dimension* focuses on the overall and specific actions that we adopt in the stock market as investors and traders that are most effective both in terms of actual outcomes (profits) and in terms of identifying the process (strategies and tactics) that are most successful. This knowledge allows us to react to market phenomena in a way that is congruent with our personalities.

The following lists will help you identify the inner and outer games of trading.

Inner	Outer
• motivation	• strategy (overall plan) organization
• beliefs	• marshaling resources
• focus	• defining outcomes operationally
• state of mind	• developing trading rules
• attitudes	• applying well defined risk management
• thoughts	
• goals	

The interdependence of the inner and outer games of trading can be illustrated as:

Inner Game	→	Outer Game	→	Outcomes
Motivation,		Strategy,		Trading results
beliefs,		trading rules,		(profit or loss)
state of mind		risk control		

IDENTIFYING YOUR PERSONAL STRENGTHS AND WEAKNESSES

It is obvious that as investors and traders, each of us has our own specific psychological motives, goals, and tolerances that need to be factored into our choice of an investment approach or trading system. In my work with market makers and proprietary traders, I routinely ask traders to identify their strengths and weaknesses so they can develop a methodology that fits their personalities. Anyone who offers you a trading approach or system that comes ready-made, one-size-fits-all, is leading you astray. To personalize your investment plan, answer each of the following ten questions:

1. What are your greatest weaknesses as a trader?
2. What are your greatest strengths as a trader?
3. What do you find most interesting about trading?
4. What do you find least interesting about trading?
5. What do you find most enjoyable about trading?
6. What do you find least enjoyable about trading?
7. How much effort (time and money) are you willing to commit to trading?
8. Is it important for you to trade by feel or intuition? Why?
9. Is it important for you to have a totally mechanical system? Why?
10. What is your ideal trading approach or system?

As you analyze your responses to each question, it should become clear to you exactly what *you* will need for your approach to be successful. If you are a trader who thrives on momentum or relies on "market feel," a mechanical system is not for you. On the other hand, if you rely too heavily on market emotion to the point where it clouds your judgment or affects operating strict risk control parameters, you may want to consider a more systematic method to increase your discipline. Understanding the specific idiosyncrasies of your personality and temperament is essential for being a mentally tough online trader.

Consider this comment from Toby Crabel, president and CEO of Crabel Capital management:

Early in 1987 I had a four month drawdown that really set me back. I questioned whether I even wanted to trade at that point. I took a year to reevaluate the whole thing. . . . In reality, the answer for me was completely moving away from discretionary trading to the point where I am today: completely systematic in my approach. It was developing the systematic approach that allowed me to eliminate the volatility; the emotional volatility and the uneven trading performance.

All successful traders at one time have had to overcome inhibiting feelings and behaviors that negatively affected their investment performance. The key for you is to identify those market attitudes and behaviors that prevent you from achieving the results you desire and substituting them with others that are positively suited to you.

7

Focusing and Managing Your State of Mind

The key to trading discipline is focus; it is knowing through experience and research what is the essential object of your attention, filtering out all external and internal interference and resistance. Top traders, like top athletes, understand this principle. Being a mentally tough online trader requires nothing less! The trader must be conditioned to react and take action at one's own particular point of focus in the stock market with decisiveness, unimpaired by conflict or uncertainty.

It is important to remember that focus is ultimately your choice and your responsibility as to what you select as your object of attention and concentration. Strong focus allows the trader to stay true to the top performing recipe:

- Identify a signal
- Take automatic action
- Feel good (resourceful, open to new opportunities)

The difficult part, of course, is maintaining a high level of focus, avoiding distraction or internal hindrance. It is for this reason that having a well defined game plan—yours—is so vital.

In the *Intuitive Trader* (Wiley, 1996), I pointed out that there is an optimal performance state for the trader that is characterized by the following:

- Physical relaxation
- Psychological calm
- Positive expectation
- Energized demeanor
- Active engagement
- Alertness
- Effortlessness
- Anxiety management
- A "sense" of being in control

An optimal performance state is, in fact, a unified experience of heightened focus, where the trader feels completely confident and automatic in his or her response.

Traders who have experienced this level of focus often refer to it as being "in the zone." They report feeling "relaxed and loose," having "an inner quiet and calmness," "intensity," "having fun and letting go."

Donald Sliter, one of the largest independent floor traders of the S&P 500, had this to say:

> I'll tell you what; I get in a zone. I'll trade thousands of S&P contracts in a day, and I'm just moving in and moving out, feeling great, eating up everything in sight . . . I get in the car in the morning and I'm juiced. I can't wait, especially on number days or on expirations. I get so pumped up some-times . . . Just the idea that each day is going to be different, that I'm in control of my own situation, my own destiny.

Linda Leventhal, a professional market maker, put it his way:

> When you're trading, I would say it's very much like being in a race or a prize fight or for that matter, on the stage. You're per-forming! You are performing all the time. And if you're not

92

paying full attention, you will get caught. You may have been out too late or maybe you partied too much or whatever. You allow yourself to become distracted. You can lose everything in one momentary lapse. Being focused is really being there!

In the *Tao of Trading* (Dearborn, 1998), I wrote about what I felt, in my judgment, to be a striking similarity between the discipline and focus required by traders and that needed in battle by Samurai warriors in ancient Japan. For the trader, as the Samurai, in the midst of the fray, there is no time to think about the proper way to launch an attack or swing the sword; it must be second nature. When it is time to act, if the knowledge is not integral—the slightest degree of hesitation results in lethal consequences. Likewise, the trader's effective action needs to be reflexive, disciplined, and rehearsed.

Consider Suzuki's description of the Samurai swordsman (*Zen and Japanese Culture*, 1959):

> The perfect swordsman takes no cognizance of the enemy's personality, no more than of his own, for he is an indifferent onlooker of the fatal drama of life and death in which he himself is the most active participant. In spite of all the concern he has or ought to have, he is above himself, he transcends the dualistic comprehension of the situation, yet he is not a contemplative mystic, he is in the thickest of the deadly combat.

Strong focus is characteristic of the optimum performance state that enhances market performance and assures mental toughness. This last point will be fully discussed in the section on state of mind that follows.

STATE OF MIND MANAGEMENT

Top trading is the result of competence and the ability to manage one's state of mind. In the stock market, creativity of thought and action projects itself effortlessly from a state of mind that is relaxed, confident, and available. It is the natural result of focus, desire, and an ongoing commitment to improve.

Your state of mind is how you are feeling at any given time, how you are relating to your world (e.g., the stock market). Your state of mind is a reflection and expression of your capability and not in any way an assessment of your ultimate ability to do well in the market. The point is that if you change your state of mind from negative to positive you increase your level of resourcefulness in the market. You allow yourself to move from a position of psychologically reduced capacity to one of optimum performance, assuming your overall approach (fundamental or technical) possesses statistical merit.

The Resourceful State of Mind

When your thinking is optimistic, your overall state of mind is resourceful.

Optimistic, resourceful, available	→ Calm mental state characterized by focus	→ High level, effective performance

The Unresourceful State of Mind

When your thinking is pessimistic, your overall state of mind is unresourceful.

Anxiety, fear, anger, negativity	→ Poor concentration feeling uptight physically and psychologically	→ Low level, ineffective performance

Another way to compare these states of mind is:

Resourceful	Unresourceful
Confident	Angry
Enthusiastic	Vengeful
Energized, intense	Disappointed
Disciplined	Frustrated
Fun loving	Depressed
Happy	Feeling stupid
Knowledgeable	Euphoric
Loving	Excited
Grateful	Lethargic
Proud	Disorganized
Organized	Indecisive
Determined	Confused
Dynamic	Anxious
Vital	Paralyzed
Proactive	Unresponsive

Your State of Mind

Answer each of the following five questions in as detailed and thoughtful a way as possible. The more you put into this exercise, the better you can devise a trading strategy that will be successful for you.

1. How much money have you lost because you haven't managed your state of mind?
2. What has been the emotional cost of not having traded in the right state of mind?
3. How much more money would you make if you always traded in a positive, resourceful state of mind?
4. How much more fun would you have if you consistently managed your state of mind?

5. How would the entire quality of your life be enhanced if you were in a peak state of mind every day?

Fully understanding your state of mind is the key to adopting competent strategies for change and, ultimately, to achieving consistently successful trading results.

Your state of mind is the aggregate of your experiences—both internal and external—at any moment in time. The trader who can shift from a limiting state to one that is fully resourceful can react "correctly" to all the market sends one's way, providing control and discipline to adopt the optimal market action.

Consider the implication of state of mind management at times when the market scares you and causes you to freeze because, for example, Dell has broken two points and you fear losing the profit, or you hesitate after your purchase of Yahoo!, watching it violate your risk points because you are afraid to realize the initial loss and now hope it will come back! Successful trading is knowing exactly what to do next in the stock market, realizing that risk is the vehicle that allows you to achieve a positive outcome. Your state of mind is therefore key to achieving a profitable result from your sound investment strategy. For many investors and traders, achieving a consistent optimal performance state, where they can effortlessly manage their state of mind, is the ongoing challenge.

In his book *Zen in the Markets* (Warner, 1992), Edward Toppel writes:

> There is something within each of us that has a power over our minds that prevents our acting according to what we have agreed is the proper course of action. That something is present in all of us and is very powerful, more powerful than anything I know . . .
>
> Those who rid themselves of their egos are rewarded greatly. They are the superstars of their fields. In the stock market rewards come in the form of profits. In the world of art masterpieces are the result. In sports the players are all-stars

and command enormous salaries. Every pursuit has its own manifestation of victory over the ego.

In *Flow: The Psychology of Optimal Experience* (HarperCollins, 1991), Mihaly Csikszentmihalyi interviewed thousands of people to discover the characteristics and qualities of the ideal performance state. He termed this state *flow*. It is an integrated experience of heightened focus and accomplishment in the moment where we feel total confidence and control. Flow is characterized by mental calmness, low anxiety, automatic and effortless action, and increased alertness and attention. The characteristics of flow include:

Physical relaxation	Automatic response
Psychological calm	Alertness
Optimism	Confidence
Energized demeanor	In control
Fun-loving	Focus
Effortlessness	Ego-free
Anxiety-free	

As you think about managing your own state of mind as a trader, consider the importance to you of being in a peak performance state.

- Are you trading while relaxed and loose?
- Do you have a sense of inner quiet and calm?
- Do you feel a high level of energy and intensity?
- When you trade, are you totally locked into the moment?
- Are you optimistic about your results?
- Are you having fun?
- Is your trading effortless?
- Is your response to market situations automatic?
- Are you highly focused?
- Are you trading with a strong feeling of confidence?
- When you are trading, do you feel in control, no matter what the market reveals?

James E. Loehr, the sports psychologist, offers a four-step program for achieving athletic excellence (Plume, 1982) that applies equally well to trading.

1. *Self-discipline.* This is the stage of commitment. Everything worthwhile begins at this level. Here's where you do whatever you need to and make whatever sacrifices are necessary to get the job done and reach your ultimate potential. Yes, it's hard work; it means giving up things you enjoy now in order to achieve a higher financial goal later!

2. *Self-control.* Loehr describes this stage thus: "As you discipline yourself, you experience steady increases in self-control of what you do, what you think, and how you react." You begin to understand market action and the way you relate to it. This ultimately provides the trader with greater confidence and real control.

3. *Self-confidence.* Self-confidence flows naturally from a commitment to self-control. Self-confidence is an unshakable belief in yourself and your abilities, your proven market techniques, and your ability to execute flawlessly. It comes from believing that you are in control and taking full responsibility for whatever happens.

4. *Self-realization.* Self-realization is living up to your full potential as a human being and as a trader. It is accepting yourself confidently and allowing yourself to think intuitively about the market. It is opening yourself consistently to all that you are capable of achieving. Famed basketball coach John Wooden described this stage well when he said, "Success is peace of mind, which is a direct result of self-satisfaction in knowing you did your best to become the best that you are capable of becoming."

It is equally important for you as a trader to learn how to condition yourself to monitor your thoughts and actions in the market. Listen to what you're saying and thinking to yourself. Develop a tolerance and friendliness in your own inner voice. Be mindful of pessimism or negativity and replace the negative talk with that which is optimistic and constructive. Do not just try to avoid bad thoughts or habits—replace them. Here are some examples of energizing thoughts:

- I always give it my best shot.
- I'm willing to pay any price to achieve my goals.
- I play to win, I don't play "not to lose"!
- I'm going to succeed and have fun while I'm learning.
- I'm in control of myself.
- I will be successful.

If you say to yourself "mistakes cannot be tolerated" or "I will never make mistakes" or "I'm going to punish myself for making that trade" (usually you end up punishing the people closest to you), you are sure to experience frustration, disappointment, and anger. It is simply not true that to be a winner you must be perfect.

A healthier and more effective attitude is the realization that in order to learn, you must make mistakes! Say to yourself "if I don't make mistakes, I simply won't learn." Develop the confidence in yourself to know that mistakes will be at a minimum when you have created a relaxed internal state.

In *The Mental Game* (New York; Viking Penguin, 1990), Loehr makes this point about tennis that applies equally well to trading:

> If losing is equated with failure, the battle of confidence cannot be won. Your motto should always be, "Win or lose, another step forward." You can find success in a losing effort when you establish clear performance goals prior to the match. You have the potential to learn much more from a loss than a victory. When you set your goals properly, your confidence can continue to grow, independent of your match's outcome.

Here are the essential characteristics of creative thought and performance that enhance a trader's performance:

- There is an optimum internal state for each trader.
- Only when the trader feels good (calm, relaxed, etc.) will performance approach optimum levels.
- Consistently high levels of successful trading performance is a direct result of the way one feels physically and psychologically while trading.
- What the trader is processing internally is within her or his control.
- Competitive and sustained trading success is the ability to create internal states of mind, regardless of market action.

The critical factors, then, leading traders to an experience of heightened creativity of thought and action are:

- A mentally and physically relaxed state of mind
- Confidence
- Optimism
- Focus on the moment
- Energized demeanor
- Elevated awareness and the ability to let go

A tight trading performance is usually the result of one of the following factors:

- Trying too hard, constantly trying to make the trade happen
- Worrying about past errors and the concomitant fear of repeating those mistakes
- Tentative or unsure execution
- Becoming overly concerned with the profit or loss; making the trading decisions cautious, anxious, or mechanical as opposed to effortless
- Obsessed with doing the "right thing"; being conscious rather than unconscious of every move you make in the market

Remember the keys to successful trading are:

- You must feel good to perform well. Your trading performance is a direct reflection of how you feel internally, not the other way around. When you feel good, you perform at high levels.
- Feeling good is in your control because you can alter your internal state.
- Trading performance at the highest levels occurs automatically and without conscious deliberation, where the right internal state has been established to support proven methods and technical skills.
- Top trading is the ability to change your emotional state, to move from left brain dominance to right brain self-realization. That will guarantee optimum trading performance and will allow you to think and act creatively.

To be successful, a trader must possess the skills necessary to create and maintain positive internal feelings, regardless of the market circumstances or situation.

8

Using Positive Imagery

As a trader, it is crucial to act on your reality—your particular point of focus. You must possess an independent-minded attitude that allows you to identify and respond to your reality and realize that all market actions you take emanate from the realization of this reality. Whatever we see in the market at any time is purely subjective, is our projection—a current reflection of our emotional and physical states. You must know the difference between an effective market reality and one that is not.

Many of us think that when we are observing the market we are sharing in a common experience with all other traders. Nothing could be further from the truth. We may be looking at the same markets but we are not seeing, hearing, or feeling the same things.

When you walk out on the street in the morning, isn't what you see different when you've had a good night's sleep from when you haven't? If you have a toothache, or lose a lot of money, or are in love, don't things look a little different too? Your "reality" is totally based on your perspective.

So, too, is your reality when you are analyzing and trading the stock market, a projection of your reality. Recently I was on an elevator and the lady standing next to me kept staring at my tie. She said, "Oh, what a great tie," and then closely inspected it. As she was leaving the elevator, she said, "They are strawberries, aren't they?"

I found this interchange most curious because there were no strawberries, only red and blue polar bears on my tie. Suppose this woman purchased some strawberries from the grocery, got home, and was consumed by a polar bear. Now, that would be a bad batch of strawberries!

The funny thing is, misperceptions happen in the stock market all the time. How many times do people mistakenly see bears when there are "really" only bulls?

PROJECTING YOUR WAY TO SUCCESS

As you think about the images you project internally, be aware that your brain is like your own movie theater; you're its principal actor, producer, and director. You can view any number of situations as you choose. In the same way, you can represent any trading experience or situation as you direct. That is why losing on a particular trade to some traders is paralyzing while to others it can be just part of the process or a source of gaining additional market information. Of course, nobody likes to lose!

As you think about the pictures, sounds, and feelings you process, consider some of the controls available to you as you are creating this mental imagery. Notice what happens as you change the imagery both visually and aurally in brightness, color, distance, volume, and duration. How you represent any single trading experience will immediately and profoundly alter your state of mind.

Bodily response	Visualization	Auditory
Body feels light, confident. Shoulders are erect, torso straight. Facial muscles taut. Breathing deep and relaxed. Eyes looking straight ahead. Feeling strong, energized, and enthusiastic.	Seeing yourself succeed. Watching yourself in control, relaxed. Looking competent, confident, and positive.	The voice of confidence. The sounds of "I knew I was right," "I have the market pegged," or "This market is doing just what I thought it would."

The Winning State of Mind

Resourceful state of mind → Strategy → Positive trading response

- Anxiety-free
- Self-trust
- Confident
- High self-esteem

Psychological Characteristics of the Winning State of Mind

- Expect the best of yourself.
- Establish a personal standard of excellence.
- Create an internal atmosphere for success based on compelling motivation and focus.
- Communicate effectively with yourself; be positive, resourceful, self-empowering.

Visual Imagery That Enhances Performance

- Picturing success
- Seeing yourself in control
- Looking competent, relaxed, confident, positive
- Viewing a positive visual image that improves your performance

Auditory Imagery That Enhances Performance

- Hearing the voice of confidence
- The sounds of "I knew I was right"
- The voice of positive expectation

Kinesthetic Imagery That Enhances Trading Performance

- Body feels light, confident
- Body is energized and strong
- Focus is direct and alert
- Breathing is relaxed, effortless, long and deep

Positive Beliefs That Enhance State of Mind

- I believe I am or will be a successful trader.
- I believe I can achieve excellent results in my trading.
- I believe I can identify and execute winning trades.
- I believe I can trade with confidence.
- I believe I can trade effortlessly and automatically.
- I believe each day's performance is fresh.
- I believe I am personally responsible for all my trading results.
- I believe I can be successful without being perfect.

- I believe my performance as a trader does not determine my self-worth.
- I believe one bad trade is just that.
- I believe trading is a process.
- I believe that by believing in myself and in any proven methodology and by approaching trading each day with a fresh, positive state of mind, I possess the ultimate trading edge.

IMPLEMENTING YOUR VISUALIZATIONS AND BELIEFS

Complete the following exercises.

Exercise 1. Write down five beliefs that you currently have about yourself that limit your market performance.

Exercise 2. Write down five beliefs about yourself that you can adopt to improve your market performance.

Exercise 3. Write down five beliefs that you currently have about the markets or trading that limit your performance.

Exercise 4. Write down five beliefs that you can adopt about trading and the markets to enhance your performance.

Exercise 5. Think of ten visual images that can instantly change your state of mind. Create an imaginary slide carousel in your mind so that you can tap into any single slide whenever you want to enhance your trading state. It can be an image of skydiving, bungee jumping, or winning a gold medal at the trading olympics.

Exercise 6. Create a mini jukebox in your mind. Think of ten songs—rock, rap, classical, and/or jazz—that you can access to change your state of mind. If the market gets you down, play a tune that will strengthen and refresh you.

OPTIMIZING YOUR VISUALIZATION

The words you choose to speak to yourself will enhance or detract from your trading state. So as you interpret the market experience to yourself, be aware not only of the words you are using but how you are using them and in what internal tonality of voice.

As you create this internal imagery, keep in mind the obvious; you are in control. Also, how you represent any single trading experience to yourself will immediately and profoundly alter your state of mind as shown below.

Comparison of Negative and Positive Self-Talk

Negative self-talk

- You are a fool, how could you have made that trade?
- What will *X* think of me?
- I hope I don't make a terrible trade again.
- Those market makers picked me off again.

Positive self-talk

- Everyone makes mistakes— move on to the next trade.
- I'm doing my best. The good trades will take care of themselves.
- Relax, exercise discipline, and make your next trade.
- I have to think more critically about where to place my stops.

Comparison of Internal Vocabulary Usage— "Feel" the Difference

Negative	Positive
Idiot	Disciplined
Crazy	Decisive
Loser	Patient
Fool	Methodical
Emotional	Consistent
Failure	Winner
Wild	Confident
Stubborn	Focused
Shooter (from the hip)	Calculated

Reenergizing Yourself

Top traders know consciously or unconsciously the importance of state of mind to successful trading. Having the ability to automatically change from a limiting to a resourceful state provides the investor and trader with the mental toughness to take losses and ride profits. They can stay confident, focused, and physically relaxed when decisions are made not out of fear or reaction but with discipline, patience, and control.

As traders and investors, we need to maintain and reenergize our mental conditioning through constant and consistent exercise and practice. Many traders, particularly novices, resist this idea. They believe trading or investing is simply an activity of numbers, charts, prices, and profit and loss statements. They avoid the difficult task of self-examination, of learning what motivates their thoughts and actions when interacting with the market.

PART 3

Technical Analysis for the Online Trader

Part 3 offers a technical analytical framework for observing market behavior in order to understand its interaction with the psychology of the individual investor. Later you will see how these concepts apply to the active online trader. The emphasis here, for both long-term and short-term traders, is understanding the importance of mental toughness at key market junctures where opportunity is greatest and anxiety and emotion are most inhibiting.

9

The Psychology of
Technical Analysis

Stock prices are not random. For our purposes, I define random as having no directional bias over time. Any trader or investor who has ever studied simple market charts can easily verify the upward or downward bias of most markets. This bias within a defined time frame is referred to as a trend. Trends can be seen as market psychology at work.

The classic definition of a trend, "higher highs and higher lows," has a strong psychological foundation. Emotionally and intellectually, there is great comfort for the investing public when a market makes new highs, falls off, and fails to make new lows in a particular period of time. Traders then become willing buyers at higher price levels and sellers are attracted to the market at even higher levels. Of course, the opposite is true for downward trending markets.

Whether the markets are trending up or down, or for that matter, not moving at all, there is an opportunity for profit. The top traders have all devised some methodology or combination of methods and techniques to trade markets with consistency. It doesn't matter if the trader is a fundamentalist or technician, each one has developed a unique "solution" to markets. This "solution" I call a trading system. It's important to understand that trading systems

113

are nothing more than an attempt to put order into a chaotic world, the world of stocks.

Having a trading system gives traders the ability to control their emotional and mental states rather than allowing their emotions to control them. A system is a disciplined method for organizing dynamic, ever-changing market phenomena.

A successful trading system is composed of a number of independent elements that are joined together to make the whole. These elements are discrete, however mutually interactive. They are:

- Trend identification
- Entry and/or exit strategies
- Money management

Remember, though, that our focus here is not on an in-depth study of the technical aspects of trading markets, but rather on how our emotional states and the psychological skills we have learned relate to using the trading system. As we have seen, it is the internal state of the trader that determines if the system or the specific analytical methods of choice will be successful.

TRENDS AND THE EFFICIENT MARKET THEORY

It would seem that if markets were really the efficient mechanisms that some academics propose, the markets would find their proper levels in one full leap. Obviously this is not the case.

Trend Identifiers

The primary methods of trend identification are:

- Linear-trendlines
- Moving averages
- Channel breakouts

Simple trendlines are usually drawn from low to low to establish an uptrend, or from high to high to establish a downtrend. (See Figure 9.1.) Variations on this method are possible by using closes instead of lows or by averaging daily ranges and using those points as references.

FIGURE 9.1 Trendline

The oldest and best-known method of establishing a trend is the moving average. (See Figure 9.2.) In its simplest form, a moving average is usually obtained by adding up a series of closes and dividing the sum by the number of days used in the series. The result is a smoothing of the series of numbers and an effective method of trend identification. Many variations are possible, such as varying the number of days in the series, using an average of the

FIGURE 9.2 Moving Average

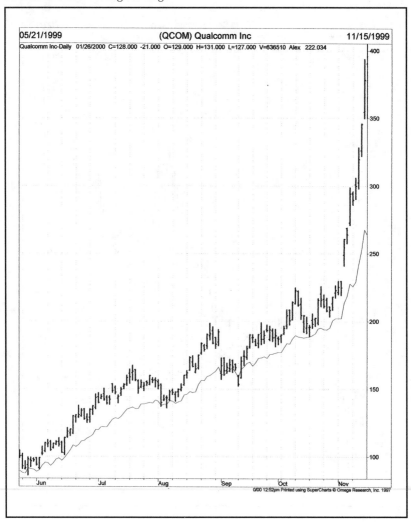

daily range, using highs or lows, and even changing the value of the most recent days compared to the oldest days. The most obvious use of the moving average is in identifying that a trend is established when the close (or whatever variable you choose) is over (or under) the average, thereby signaling direction.

The channel breakout method can be used on its own or in conjunction with the other methods. (See Figure 9.3.) I define a

FIGURE 9.3 Channel

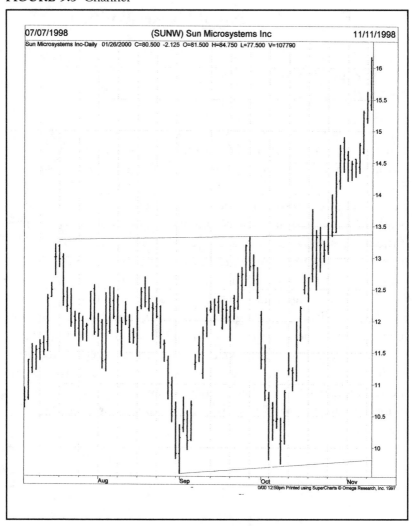

channel as a series of days or weeks that is contained within an area of highs and lows (or average of highs and lows). When a market moves through an area which has been established over a period of time, it signals a trend.

The point to remember is that the individual trader's inclination and personal psychology limits the potential use of the above concepts of trend identification. Of course, the opposite is also true.

Entry and/or Exit of Market Positions

- Fast moving averages
- Highs and lows
- Retracement

Once a trend has been identified, the trader must decide how best to enter the market. One commonly used device is the fast moving average. (See Figure 9.4.) A fast moving average is an average that is composed of a relatively short number of days or weeks. Because it responds quickly to market movement, I have labeled it "fast." A simple use of this average is to enter the market if the price is above the fast average and has already established an uptrend. An option is to buy the market as it comes to the fast average and exit the market when it violates this point.

The use of highs and lows is common among traders. When a trend is established, new highs or new lows can signal resumption of market movement in the direction of the trend. (See Figure 9.5.)

Some traders prefer to wait for the market to retrace its move to either the area of the trend change or to the moving average, or the trendline. There are many variations available to allow a trader to incorporate the concept of retracement into a system. (See Figure 9.6.)

FIGURE 9.4   Fast Moving Average

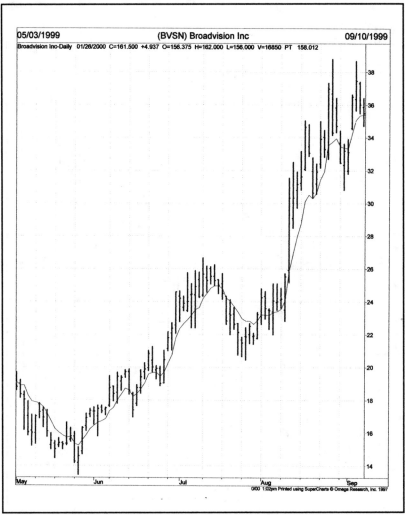

MONEY MANAGEMENT

Proper money management technique is the most difficult element of a trading system, but the most vital for success. It is possible that a system built without money management in it, even one that

FIGURE 9.5 New Highs in a Trend

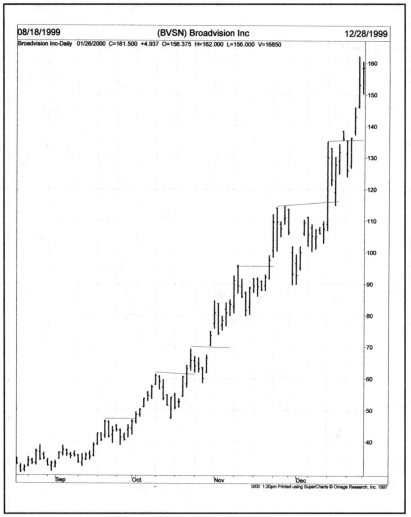

is 90 percent accurate, can wipe out your equity. The most common emotional and psychological barriers that prevent trading success stem from poor money management. All the top traders I have interviewed have come to terms with the concept of equity management and have developed a consistent methodology to deal with it.

FIGURE 9.6   Retrace to Trendline

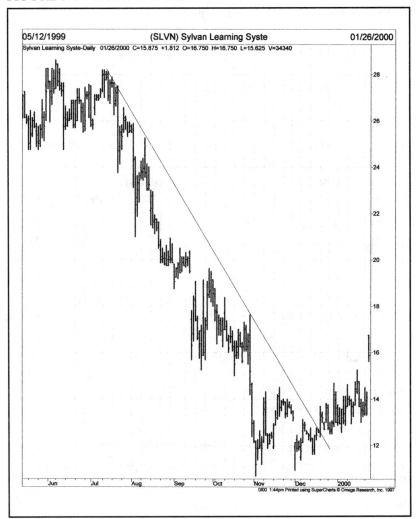

Opportunity in the stock market derives from understanding and utilizing proper money management. Too few traders acknowledge this and fewer still incorporate any methodology to protect themselves from disaster.

Many of the axioms I have listed earlier deal with the concept of money management. For example,

- Take small losses, let your profit run.
- Don't let a profit turn into a loss.
- Don't risk all your equity on a single trade.

The following table illustrates the rationale for many of these axioms by showing the mathematics of money management.

Equity	Losses at 500	Net loss	Profit at 1500	Net Profit	Net Result
10,000	6 losses =	3000	4 profits =	6000	3000
10,000	7 losses =	3500	3 profits =	4500	1000
10,000	8 losses =	4000	2 profits =	3000	(1000)

As you can see in the above table, a system designed to take small losses and large profits will provide a positive result even if it is correct only three out of ten trades. If the system runs into a series of eight out of ten losses, the equity drawdown is still relatively small. You do not need a specific formula for arriving at optimum risk/reward ratios. A 3:1 or 4:1 risk to reward ratio, over time, will serve the trader or investor very well.

Understanding the key elements that are necessary to build a trading system gives us the framework in which we can exploit market opportunities. It allows us to utilize the psychological skills we have learned that complement the individual requirements of our personalities.

I am reminded of the story of the trader who sat in a boardroom with several other traders and boasted of a most unusual system. This trader would carry an empty Coke bottle around and every so often put it to his ear, claiming that he was receiving buy and sell instructions from aliens in a spaceship from outer space. When the trades turned out correct he basked in the glow of success, telling anyone who would listen about his good fortune and alien friends. However, when the trades were unsuccessful he would quickly get out of the position and claim that sunspot interference caused distortions that made him misunderstand the instructions from his alien friends.

The elements of this system were devilishly simple. He made a trade, took large profits and small losses. It's certainly one way to trade, though not one I recommend!

10

Chart Analysis
and Trends

The simple uptrend line in Figure 10.1 graphically illustrates the "higher highs, higher lows" definitions of an uptrend. The trendline is drawn from a low to the next low and carried forward to await the price movement over time. After the fact, the trendline appears to be remarkably successful for so simple a concept.

Whether the trendline itself becomes a self-fulfilling prophecy or it really is a linear representation of the trend is not important. How we can profit from this repeated market action is our focus. The trendline can be successful consistently except for one thing— the psychological barriers that prevent most of us from using this device with consistency and discipline. Let's examine what is happening and how we might create a method to use the trendline.

After we have drawn a trendline, the opportunity to use it comes as the market is falling into it and allows the trader to buy a breaking market. Psychologically, buying the market at this stage requires three things.

1. Belief in the area of the line
2. Confidence to buy when everyone is selling
3. Accepting the possibility that you may be wrong and will be forced to take a loss

FIGURE 10.1   Defined Uptrend

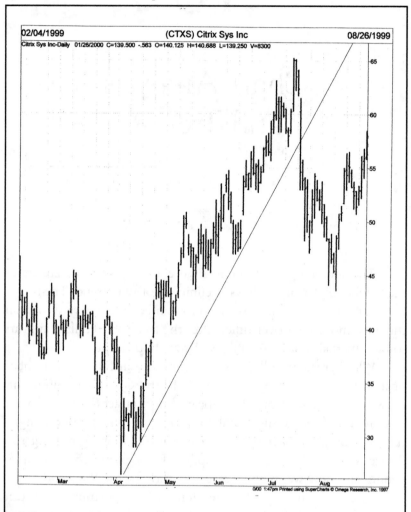

What is required here is to refocus how we see this opportunity. If I develop a simple trading system using all the elements stated above, I can determine the trend with points one and two and place a buy at point three. The first psychological barrier is buying at or near the trendline you determined. The second psychological barrier is deciding when to exit the market. This is the most difficult to deal with. You must shift your focus from "they are going to get me out" to "it's better to take a small loss knowing this trade has defined risk and unlimited upside potential."

A number of things happen when we employ this strategy. The first is we preserve our equity. The second is we have no position and should be able to make a more objective decision about the market in the future. By conditioning ourselves to utilize this discipline on a consistent basis, we allow for opportunities where profits will run later.

Another element that we can introduce into our system is reentry. I have found that one of the reasons traders hesitate to get out of a market is that they harbor a fear that they will be taken out of the market and they will never be able to reenter.

The reentry puts you back into the market. If, for example, our reentry is based on the trendline, we will reestablish our positions as soon and as often as the market satisfies our criteria. These simple elements of a trading system will be refined, adjusted, and fine tuned over time. But whatever approach we employ, we must be consistent!

I know there are those traders who will focus on the market breaking the trendline, signaling a change of direction. Great! However, bear in mind the approach is the same. The trendline gives us a lot of information and we must respect the market's ability or inability to hold it. One of my favorite situations is a close under an established trendline that is immediately followed by a close above that very line. This is a high percentage, defined risk, buy signal. Here is a market that has violated its uptrend line, chasing weak longs and attracting short sellers. The market's inability to follow through, reverse, and resume its course—shaking out weak shorts and attracting new longs—signals a very clear buying opportunity.

The analytical possibilities that exist when employing a trendline in moving markets are limited only by the trader's imagination. The same holds true with moving averages. A moving average is a nonlinear representation of a trendline. The moving average gives the trader the ability to define what constitutes a trend and allows him or her to further personalize a trading system. By changing the number of closes in the series, the trader will change how quickly the average responds to changes in the market. As the market moves over the average and continues away from it, a trend is in place. How the trader uses the elements of a system to operate effectively in that trend is based on personal levels of conviction, confidence, and the trader's own state of mind.

The most difficult market to trade is the one with no trend at all. However, a market that is not trending, with no upward or downward bias, may be said to be in a sideways trend. This trend creates additional opportunities and profitable strategies can be devised. As we will see later in a discussion about support and resistance, market psychology plays an important role in creating this sideways trend—also called a channel. (See Figure 10.2.)

As a market moves to a level that attracts buyers, it will soon stabilize and trade away from a price near where sellers become more reluctant to sell. The rally peaks when sellers who were attracted by the higher prices and weak or short-term longs begin to exit. The market then retreats to the previous lows, where the process repeats itself. This market action can be repeated for days, weeks, months, or years. One opportunity resides in first determining that the market is in a channel and then creating a system to profit from it.

Another approach is to wait for the upper or lower boundaries of the channel to be penetrated, thus signaling a significant change in direction. The ability of the market to move out of the channel indicates a change in market psychology. In an upside breakout, sellers now find themselves overwhelmed by aggressive buyers who are willing to pay higher prices. The opposite is true for a downside breakout. When either of these events occur, the trader's trend-following rules are the keys that open the lock of market opportunity.

SUPPORT AND RESISTANCE—
FEAR, GREED, AND HOPE

It's fear, greed, and hope that create this channel market pattern.

The pattern described above is a good example of support and resistance. It's easy to see the dynamics of the market as it repeatedly holds the lows and highs over an extended period of time.

FIGURE 10.2 Channel

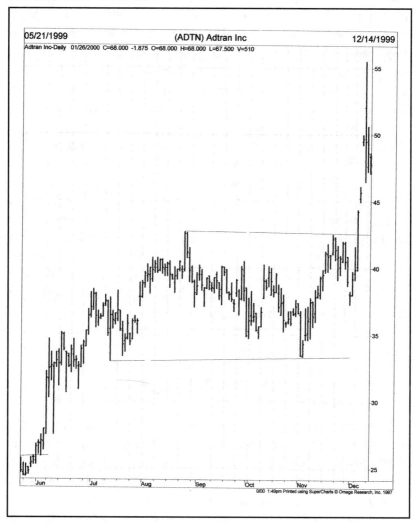

Now let's examine what is taking place as the market breaks out of the channel, in the Figure 10.2 example, on the upside. Aggressive buying and shortcovering drives the market to a point that attracts new sellers and profit-taking longs. This begins the market's normal retracement. However, as the market moves back toward the area of the top of the channel, we can examine the forces at play. Former buyers—or potential buyers who saw the market move through the channel highs and missed the opportunity—begin to buy again near those highs. At the same time, short sellers who did not exit quickly enough now see the opportunity to buy back their positions close to their entry point. This combined buying at the channel high area establishes support. Similarly a breakdown below the channel lows and subsequent rally forms resistance. Each of these occurrences is an opportunity to enter the market in the direction of the trend with reduced risk.

A variation on this idea of channel support and resistance is the trendline support or resistance. After a trendline has been broken, a retracement back to the trendline forms support or resistance. (See Figure 10.3.) One of the more reliable patterns I have seen is called the "fan." (See Figure 10.4.) This pattern is usually three trendlines and retracements, which precedes a substantial move. The same market psychology recurs at higher and higher levels where the market doesn't retrace at all.

RETRACEMENTS

One of the more difficult aspects of trading for many traders is to develop the confidence to buy a breaking market or to sell a market rally. Of course, in our discussion we're assuming a trend has been established. We have seen above that support and resistance areas offer some benchmarks or reference points.

There is another trading method to take advantage of the market's normal retracements. Markets tend to retrace a third, a half, or two thirds of the previous move. Many traders get caught up in exact numbers (e.g., .382, .684, etc.) and forget that a few ticks is not meaningful in a dynamic and fluid marketplace. If a market retraces 50 percent of a previous move and shows signs of finding support, then the trader has a lot of information with which to make a high percentage, low risk trade.

FIGURE 10.3   Support at Trendline

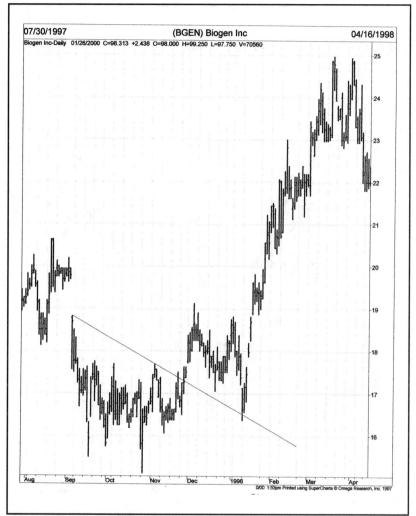

I have now demonstrated a few tangible ways to follow the famous axiom "buy low, sell high" to success and profits. You can look for retracement breaks or rallies that are near support or resistance, and are a significant percentage of the previous move, in order to enter the market.

May the axioms be with you!

131

FIGURE 10.4 Trendline Fan

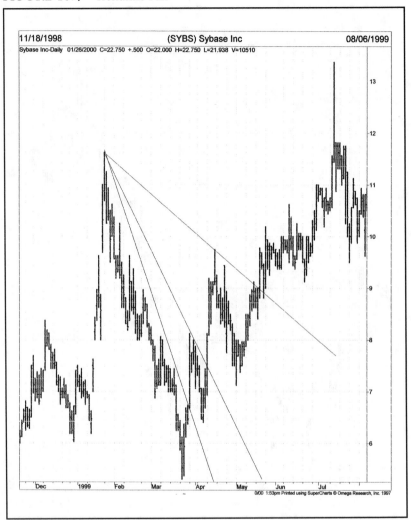

11

More about Trends

A discussion about trends is important because all the top traders I have spoken to seem to know or believe they know where the markets are, relative to the trend. For example, the market is bottoming, topping, retracing, etc.

Each major up or down trend has three phases. They are:

1. Accumulation
2. Main phase
3. Distribution

The accumulation phase of a market is characterized by low prices, light volume, small open interest, and small daily ranges. On occasion, the market might have a flurry of activity, but it quickly reverts to the doldrums. This is a period when everything about the market seems negative or uninteresting. Downside becomes limited as buyers begin to establish positions and sellers await better prices. As the market rallies away from the bottom, some weak longs and expectant sellers put a lid on the market, which gives the buyers more opportunity. This continues until the market enters the next phase.

The main phase begins with a breakout and a sustained rally above the bottom area. (See Figure 11.1.) No apparent fundamental change or increased public awareness has caused this rally, and trading has expanded but is not volatile. During this phase the reasons

FIGURE 11.1 Breakout above Accumulation

for the trend become more public and trading interest increases. Volatility and daily ranges expand and the public at large is now convinced of higher prices. This leads to the third phase.

Long-term buyers who accumulated this market near the lows use the public excitement to liquidate their long positions. This is the distribution phase. It is marked by large swings in the market, record open interest, high volume, and media interest. It's the beginning of a reversal.

Reversal Patterns

Traders who don't learn from history will continue to buy tops and sell bottoms.

The chart patterns that are created by trader psychology during accumulation and distribution are called reversal patterns: a visual representation of fear and greed playing themselves out in a constant struggle. (See Figure 11.2.) These patterns are seen time and time again. Rounded bottoms and tops, "V" or spike bottoms and tops, double or triple bottoms or tops, and head and shoulders bottoms and tops are the most common reversal chart patterns. Bottoms usually are quieter and take a longer time to develop, but on occasion a spike or double bottom occurs in a short period of time as the market extends beyond an expected low.

Tops, on the other hand, are more often than not volatile, quick to form, and accompanied by lots of noise and attention. (See Figure 11.3.)

One interesting chart pattern is that of the reversal day. Sometimes called a "key reversal," it is a high or contract high followed by a lower close for the day or week. This market action usually typifies weak buying by longs and short covering by sellers who cover on the new highs. When this buying is exhausted, the market is vulnerable and falls. This action may or may not signal a top but is a high percentage pattern for a continuation of the break.

FIGURE 11.2   Reversal Patterns

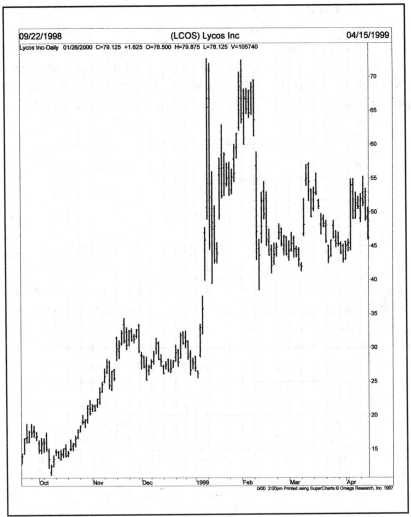

Continuation Patterns—Midlife Crises

This pattern is like midlife. It can be stressful and confusing. Continuation patterns generally present themselves halfway through the trend.

FIGURE 11.3 Top Pattern

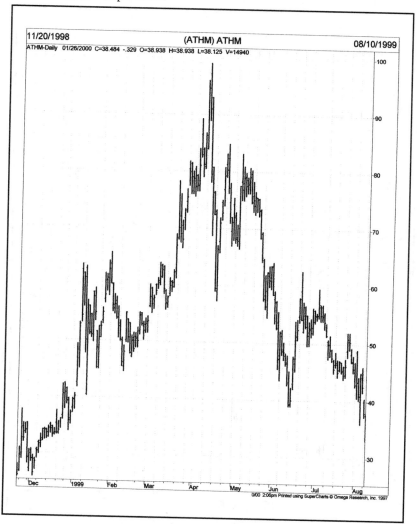

During the main phase of a trending market, certain patterns develop repeatedly. I call these continuation patterns because they usually are mere pauses in the established trend. Their names are indicative of their shapes: triangles, flags, and rectangles. (See Figure 11.4.)

FIGURE 11.4   Continuation Patterns

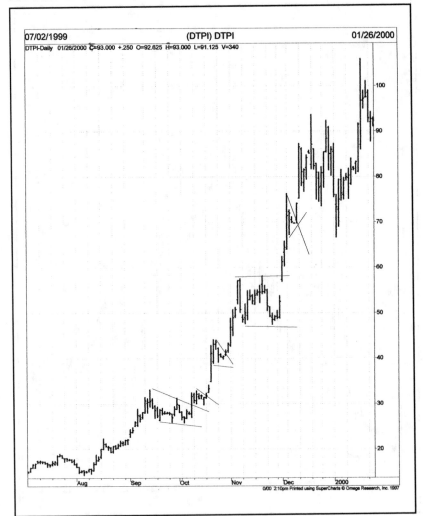

After a market moves significantly in one direction it tends to pause as those attracted by the run up and short-term longs responding to their profits begin to sell. This sell-off finds support and begins its climb to the high of this move, but falls short as more sellers take advantage of the rally. This next break finds buyers at a higher level than the last sell-off did and another rally begins, only to be met by sellers at a lower level than the last rally high. This tug-of-war over a few days or weeks begins to form one of three basic triangles:

1. Symmetrical triangle, so-named because of the similar ascending and descending lows and highs
2. Ascending triangle, so-named because of the higher lows and equal highs
3. Descending triangle, so-named because of the lower highs and equal lows

Traders can use this pattern in various ways. Buying the reaction to the low end of the triangle offers an opportunity to enter with the trend or, as some traders like to do, buy on the breakout over the trendline drawn from one triangle high to the next triangle high, or a new high for this move.

Flags are similar patterns except that they are formed by lower highs and lower lows. Many traders make the mistake of buying a market during this pattern and using a new low as a stop area. If you are confident that you are in a continuation pattern, you must assume that this could be a flag and expect a new low. It's the weak longs and over-anxious short sellers who set this pattern up.

Rectangles are channels created by equal highs and lows and as the market is again tugged at in turn by buyers and sellers in a fixed range. (See Figure 11.5.)

The point to remember is that one's psychological skills of enhanced belief and confidence are what enable personal involvement in the market at these times.

Gaps

Gaps, price action that produces a higher low than the previous high or a lower high than the previous low, are important indica-

FIGURE 11.5 Rectangle Patterns

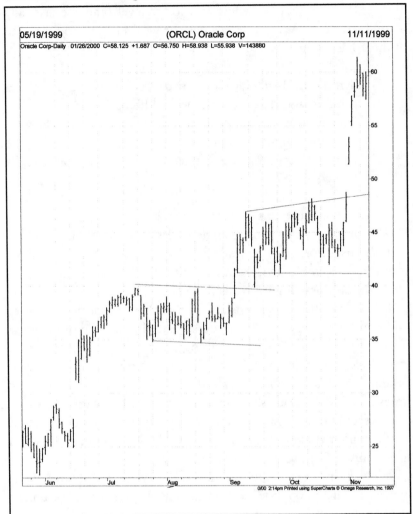

tors of the market strength or weakness. (See Figure 11.6.) There are four types of gaps:

1. Common gap
2. Breakaway gap

FIGURE 11.6 Gaps

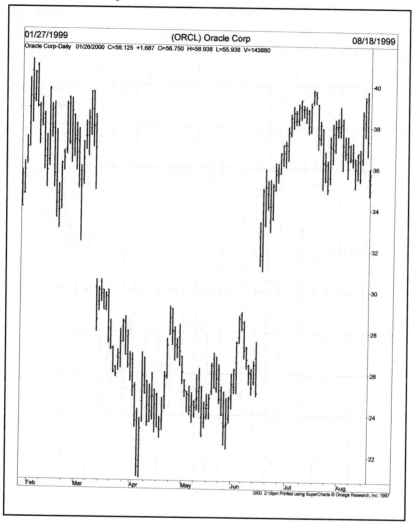

3. Runaway gap
4. Exhaustion gap

The common gap appears inside a larger formation such as a channel or triangle and does not have much significance. The breakaway gap gets its name because it usually occurs when a market is moving through important support or resistance areas of trendlines. (See Figure 11.7.) If a market closes near a resistance area but not above it and the next day opens sharply higher, it creates a gap. The market now has an area where no trading has taken place and it poses additional questions to traders. Those traders who sold against

FIGURE 11.7 Breakaway Gap

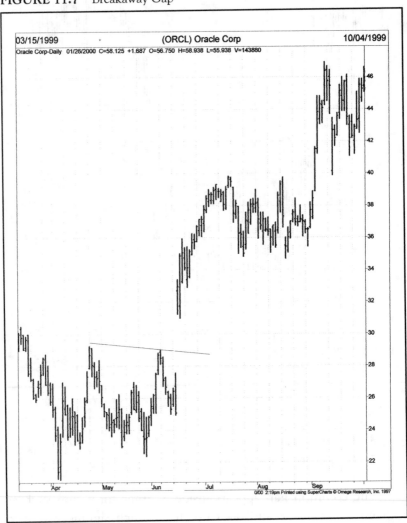

the previous highs must now decide whether to cover at much higher levels than they had anticipated, or to wait for a market retreat back to the area of previous highs. On the other hand, potential longs must decide whether to wait for the retracement or to join the already aggressive buying that is taking place. This scenario sets up the age-old question about the importance of "filling in" the gap retracement to a former support area. If the market is very strong, then the gap may be partially filled or not filled at all. Some traders focus on the idea that a filled-in gap shows market weakness. I believe that analysis of subsequent action is essential in determining if the market is still in the uptrend.

A runaway gap occurs most often from a continuation pattern and is sometimes called a "measuring gap" because the subsequent move's objective is about the size of the previous move to the continuation pattern. (See Figure 11.8.)

The exhaustion gap occurs after sharp and volatile moves and sometimes in a series of two or three. (See Figure 11.9.) A most interesting result of an exhaustion gap is the "island reversal." (See Figure 11.10.) This is formed by an exhaustion gap followed by another gap in the opposite direction, leaving the top day or week looking like an island. This pattern has a high reliability and quite often signals long-term tops and bottoms.

Summary of Gaps

These gap patterns, as well as the various technical formations I have discussed, comprise the language with which the market gives the trader information. But what is most important is this: It is necessary for the trader to effectively communicate this information to himself or herself, and to be psychologically able to utilize this information to produce winning results.

FIGURE 11.8 Measuring Gap

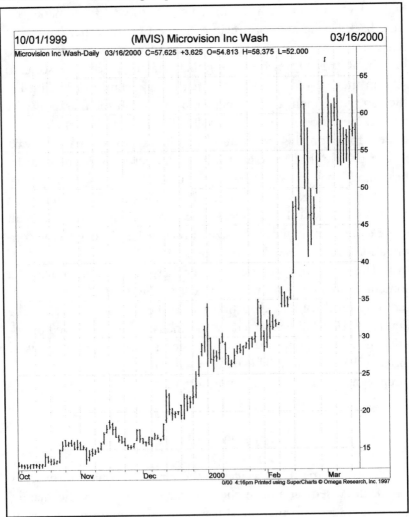

OVERCOMING PSYCHOLOGICAL
BARRIERS TO TRADING

There are many books that concentrate on technical analysis
for developing systems and utilizing specific technical strategies and

FIGURE 11.9   Exhaustion Gap

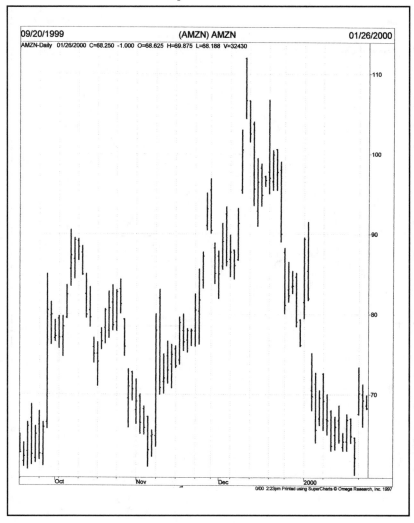

techniques. This chapter offers information on how to overcome the psychological barriers that routinely confront the trader at the moment of decision at critical junctures in the market. The trader can overcome inhibiting psychological pressures by maintaining defined objectives, clarity of focus, and a consistently resourceful state of

FIGURE 11.10 Island Reversal

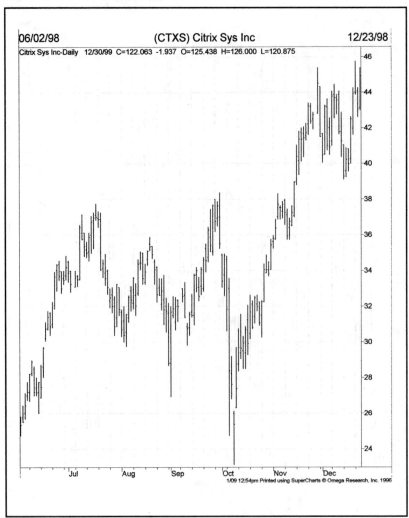

mind. Successful trading has more to do with knowing how to adapt your psychological makeup to a specific market strategy than with possessing any particular trading system.

12

Active Online Trading

It serves us well to remember that personalized trading systems provide traders with the ability to trade by using logic rather than emotion. The stock market is a huge marketplace with well over 9,000 individual stocks from which to choose. In the following sections, I present many ideas, patterns, setups, and approaches to active online trading (from one day to several weeks). Trading in shorter time frames is not for everyone! In fact, most short-term traders are not successful. However, many are successful and the reason they are is that they combine mental toughness with solid methodology based on research and sound money management.

The portfolio of stocks that you choose to trade is critical. Serious consideration must be given that their selection fits short-term trading.

STOCK SELECTION CRITERIA

The following should be your basic stock selection criteria:

- Liquidity
- Volatility
- Sponsorship
- Information
- Price level

Liquidity

Position traders have the luxury of slowly accumulating a favored stock, even if the daily volume and participation are light. Short-term trading requires selecting stocks that have a trading following and therefore usually have depth in bids and offers throughout the day. It can be quite frustrating to have bought a thinly traded stock just right but see the potential profit disappear because there are no immediate bids to take you out of the market.

Volatility

Successful trading requires movement. Selecting your favorite long-term stock as a trading vehicle isn't the answer. A good stock for trading is a stock that usually moves in a wide daily range. This doesn't mean you have to restrict yourself to high-priced flyers or the news-of-the-day stock. Many stocks at different price levels will provide you a fair opportunity for profit over a day or two. No one, other than you, should select the stock for you to trade. Part of gaining an edge is being independently focused on a stock and analyzing the way it moves. Because one particular stock is not active all the time, selecting one dozen or two dozen stocks to watch should provide you with frequent opportunity.

Sponsorship

Your portfolio selection should be fluid. Stocks move in and out of favor continuously. Focusing on some obscure company that you know will wake up some day is, in my opinion, a waste of time. Investing in dull stocks that have little movement or no financial industry sponsorship are a lost opportunity and a waste of your trading resources.

Information

Stocks that move and have sponsorship usually are in the news or are widely discussed. Analyst research, rumor, merger, or a "story" creates information that helps in making many trading decisions.

Price Level

Many traders select stocks on the basis of price. This is the wrong approach because the short-term trader is interested in movement. Yes, it's true that a $20 stock that moves a point or so has a larger percentage move than does a $50 stock moving a point or so. However, the probability of the $20 stock giving you the move you need in the short term is so small that you should look elsewhere. If the size of your trading capital is not sufficient to trade 1,000 shares of a $50 or $100 stock, then trade 100 shares or even 50 shares to maintain a trader's edge.

In the following sections I concentrate on concepts specifically associated with short-term trading. Until recently, only two approaches allowed participation in the stock market. For most people in or out of the financial community, investing for the long term was the accepted method. Short-term trading or market making was the sole province of industry insiders, who were able to maintain an edge by making access to the market very difficult.

Even though, as described previously, the public now has equal access to the markets, I believe the best opportunity for active trading success lies in the swing trade. For most people, the intense concentration and discipline required to scalp for ⅛, ¼, or ½ point are difficult at best to master. The competition from insiders, who have engaged in scalping for years, and even from newcomers, is formidable.

There is, however, a trading niche that makes more sense. In between the scalper or market maker and the large players who enter the market for longer time frames is the swing trader. Market makers supply liquidity by scalping the spread between high bids and low offers, and longer-term players put on positions for weeks or months.

The opportunities lie in the movement of stocks over a full day or over two or three days. These moves are difficult for the large investors because large investors can't move in and out without affecting their own position. In fact, the pattern, ideas, and setups discussed here are the result of the interplay between the market maker and the long-term trader. The natural ebb and flow of price movement that we witness day in and day out offer us our greatest opportunities. Although not technical analysis in the classic sense, what follows here are patterns and setups designed to put you into a low-risk trade and get you out of that trade in a short period of time.

TRADING PATTERNS

All of the trading patterns discussed below fall into one of the following three categories:

1. Breakout trades
2. Retracement trades
3. Tests

Breakout Trades

Breakout trades occur after a period of consolidation (see Figure 12.1), after setups such as an inside day (see Figure 12.2), or after a constricted-range day (see Figure 12.3). Entry in the break-

FIGURE 12.1 Breakout of Consolidation

FIGURE 12.2   Breakout after Inside Day

out trade is usually not as advantageous as in other categories, but entering the market in what appears to be a strong directional bias can make up for that.

FIGURE 12.3   Breakout after Constricted Days

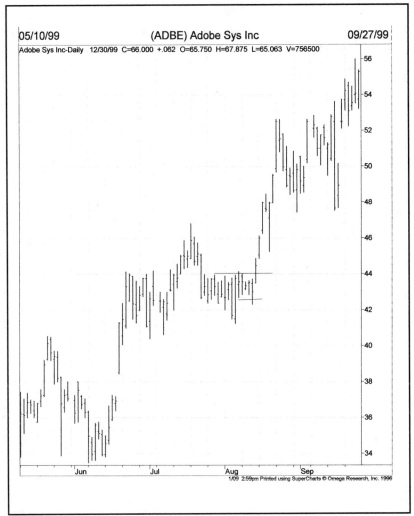

Retracement Trades

Retracements occur in the context of a trend. Buying on a pullback in an uptrend by using a percentage retracement such as 50 percent (see Figure 12.4), a moving average, or a trendline (see Figure 12.5) helps define the risk.

FIGURE 12.4 50 Percent Retracement

Tests

The market is constantly testing previous price levels: two-day lows or double bottoms and tops. (See Figure 12.6.) Here again is a low-risk opportunity to enter the market. Remember, these trades

FIGURE 12.5 Retracement to Trendline

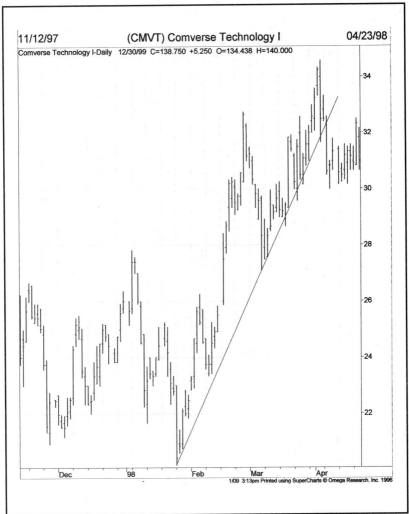

are low risk because they are based on defined entry points with circumscribed risk.

Each of these types of patterns and setups occurs in time frames from 5 minutes to weekly. My personal preference is a daily time

FIGURE 12.6 Tests

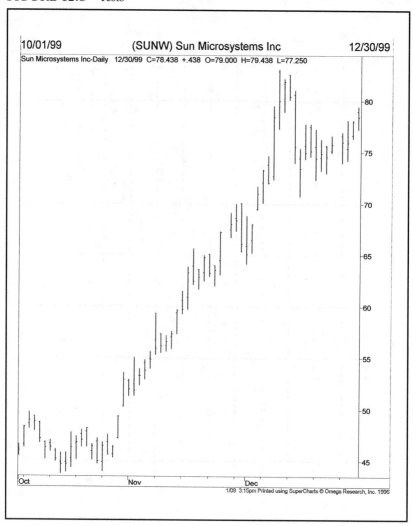

frame for most stocks and a 30-minute time frame for some of the more volatile stocks.

Short-term trading telescopes all market movement and behavior into a self-imposed time requirement that enlarges and distorts the impact of the market on the trader's emotional state of mind.

Therefore, day trade swing trading demands organization of thought, discipline of action, and commitment to allow numerous trading decisions to be made in the face of possibly suffering repeated losses.

All successful traders have tenacity and a belief in themselves. Although their methods or systems differ, their approach and state of mind are remarkably similar. Mental toughness is their edge.

13

Technical Considerations for Swing Trading

The necessary technical ingredients for a successful approach to swing trading are not unlike those necessary for longer time frames. They include:

- Trend identification
- Market entry point
- Market exit point
- Money management

Trend Identification

You may be asking yourself why you need trend identification specifically for shorter time frames. The answer is that markets exhibit consistent characteristics in uptrends, downtrends, or sideways moves. For example, it's almost axiomatic that buying lower openings in a bull market is a high probability trade. So, too, is selling higher openings in a bear market.

Trends, however, have many time frames and the swing trader can incorporate and capitalize on each one that can be identified. I like to break trends down to three workable areas. The intermediate-term trend, usually three to ten days, is derived from what most traders see as the long-term trend of the market. The short-term trend, which lasts from two to five days, can be in the direction of the intermediate-term trend or a reaction to it. And the daily trend can result from the setup from the previous day or two of an overnight news event, or of the morning government report.

In my business partner's proprietary trading system, Howard Abell honed the number of computer-generated numbers to just a few, which we use to identify the various trends in each time frame and which also creates support and resistance levels within those time frames. I believe strongly in the KISS (Keep It Simple, Stupid) philosophy of trading: the simpler the better. So now that we have determined our trend in each time frame, we must decide on entry.

Market Entry Point

Without a plan of action, that is, without knowing where the market is in relation to where it has been, the tendency of traders to react to the emotions of the market and get caught up in the crowd increases. In simple terms, this often results in buying the highs and selling the lows, a common, painful experience! In short-time frame trading, efficient entry can be the difference between a missed market, a smaller profit, or a larger-than-necessary loss.

By planning several potential entry scenarios that fit into your system, you prepare yourself for opportunities that the market offers. The most difficult thing for most novice traders to do is to buy the market as it comes crashing down to your point, number, or area. Planning and a conviction in your proven method will put you into that market. Buying a hard break or selling a sharp rally to your preplanned point is usually the smallest risk trade you can make. This applies also for buying or selling a breakout. You generally know right away if your buy or sell is a good one and, if it isn't, whether it has the least dollar risk attached to it.

Personally, I try to determine if the market is set up to buy a break; to sell a rally; or, if it's in a breakout mode, to follow strength or weakness. I then place entry orders in anticipation. This requires patience.

Many times swing trading appears like running for a crowded elevator whose doors are just beginning to close. Forget it! Remember there will be another one along in a minute. It's important to get into the elevator that will arrive at your floor, and that leads us successfully to our trading exit. Mental toughness involves both the ability to be patient and to act decisively at critical market junctures: entry, exit, and reentry points.

Market Exit Point

Steve Conners, an investment adviser and author of the book *Investment Secrets of a Hedge Fund Manager* (Probus, 1995), writes, "I want my stop hit!" He emphasized this point by trailing his stop loss orders on profitable trades so close to the market that it almost guaranteed he would be stopped out, forcing him to take his money. The same attitude goes for the stop loss order placed on losing trades. Nothing is so wasteful to a trader as a market that wallows in a no-man's-land between a small profit or no profit and a small loss. Pat Arbor, former chairman of the Chicago Board of Trade, tells a story in *The Outer Game of Trading* (Irwin, 1994) about Everett Clip, one of the senior members of the Board of Trade:

> Everett will take a new trader and march him right down to the middle of the bond pit, and he'll say, "Now, watch this." And he'd say, "What's the market?" "Five bid at six sellers," someone says. Everett would say to the new trader, "Watch very closely." He then turns to the guy who gave him the market, "I'll sell you one at five and I'll buy one from you at six." Then he turns back to the young trader and says, "You see what I just did?" The young trader would kind of look, his eyes wide

open, and say, "Yeah, you just lost a tick." Everett then says triumphantly, "That's right. Never forget it!" You see, that's how you take a loss, dispassionately, no emotion. If you can learn that, you'll be a successful trader.

If you're a short-term trader you must take the small loss and move on with your business!

Taking profits, on the other hand, is another matter. A sound approach should include price or some other objective for the market's performance. A reasonable price objective will vary with the volatility and risk of each individual market. For example, many systems created for trading stocks reduce the risk to between ⅜ and ⅝ of a point. Under those circumstances, trying to squeeze two points out of the market might be a little greedy. In other words, reward should have some relationship to risk taken. There are other objectives to consider: How quickly does the market move in your favor after you enter? Something can be said for instant gratification. Also, how does the market perform as it moves toward your price objective? Is it making a new high, then backing off, and then making another new high? Or did it go into a fast market condition but fall short of your price objective in the middle of the day? Reacting correctly and quickly to these differences can add profit dollars to any system you are using.

Money Management

Many traders confuse risk management with money management. Risk management is what we have talked about above. It is taking small losses and managing the rewards as they relate to the risks taken. Money management refers to the proper use of capital, which includes using it for maximum benefit and preserving it for maximum longevity. It makes as little sense to commit $100,000 to day trading and then trade just 100 shares, for example, as it does to trade 10,000 shares, which is too many. There is a balance to be arrived at through careful consideration of your personal comfort level, risk parameters of each system, and the volatility of the market being traded. Keep in mind that short-term trading is like hitting singles and doubles and stealing bases to win baseball games. You can win a lot of games that way, but only if you have a good defense.

Whatever method, approach, or system you create for short-term trading, you must resolve several important issues if you are to be successful. The market must be viewed as a vehicle or tool from which your objective is to extract profits. Entering the market on your terms is your edge and reduces risk to the smallest possible level. However, as important as your entry into the market is, taking the money when it's available is a close second in importance. Trying to turn a swing trade into a home run will doom you to failure. Don't mix time frames. You can't make a trade based on a five-minute chart and validate turning that trade into a position. Your short-term trading goal is to enter the market with a small risk, take your profit, and move on to the next opportunity. Worrying about what you might be leaving on the table will distort your focus and inhibit you from making good decisions. You'll find more opportunity in the markets from a sound approach or system than you'll be able to take advantage of.

Another issue you must come to terms with is the sheer number of trades you will have to make as part of your process. Believe it or not, this is a real problem for many people. Whether it is the constant decision making or the flow of paper or a stream of losses, many people fold under the weight. This goes for pit traders as well. A clearing firm in Chicago assists traders on the floor of their exchanges by teaching a proven method of scalping in the trading pit by trading for the smallest of increments throughout the trading day. The first thing traders are taught is to "scratch," or buy and sell at the same price, which teaches the traders to enter and exit the market quickly to protect themselves if the market turns. But the most important aspect of this lesson is neither of these.

The real lesson for traders is in forcing them to make trades. Yes, they must learn just to make the trades! Even when the cost of a scratch is measured in pennies, many novice traders will spend a full trading day with less than a handful of trades on their trading cards. You have to force them to enter and exit the market many times a day. I'm not suggesting that an off-floor trader should or could trade for very small increments, but the psychological barriers to making the trades are the same as for large increments.

In the following pages I demonstrate, in detail, my particular approach to swing trading. I say approach because I believe that the essential ingredient to a successful trading method is not the system but what the trader brings to that system. By approach I mean the attitudes, emotions, focus, and state of mind that the trader incorporates into whatever system or method he or she uses. As with my partner, Howard Abell, my earliest training in trading was in classic chart analysis, and I really believe in keeping it simple. That is why, except for a few computer-generated numbers that define the market's trend and create some support and resistance areas, my primary tool is the simple daily bar chart. Most of what you read here will apply in any time frame. These ideas have been put to use over many years as a professional market maker on the trading floor and in front of a screen.

TRADING METHOD

The following are some personal axioms that are integral to a successful short-term trading method:

- Patience is your edge.
- Good trades result from a high percentage of setups.
- Anticipation of market opportunities is critical.
- Predetermined buy and sell areas must be executed.
- Trade one setup per stock per day.
- Ignore the noise and follow the signal.
- Take "fast market" or climax condition profits.
- Abandon dull or nonperforming stocks.

Patience Is Your Edge

Patience and preparation serve to create an edge that helps build and conserve equity. Knowing what you expect the market to do and waiting patiently for the market to come to you—in other words, to meet your expectations—gives you that edge.

Good Trades Result from High Percentage Setups

Each day must be viewed in a larger context, which might be one day to two weeks of market action. Understanding how markets set up to make predictable moves and anticipating these moves through the setup is a valuable key to success.

Anticipation of Market Opportunities Is Critical

In most instances, waiting for the stock to demonstrate what appears to be a trading opportunity will result in entering too late for maximum profits.

Predetermined Buy and Sell Areas Must Be Executed

For those traders who have difficulty "pulling the trigger," putting resting orders in the market will get you into the trade.

Trade One Setup Trade Per Stock Per Day

Overtrading comes from indecision and anxiety. By setting your sights on one good setup in a stock, you avoid trading your emotions.

Ignore the Noise and Follow the Signal

Much of what a market does during the day can be considered noise, that is, market action without meaning. Hanging on every tick can be a wearisome and misleading chore. You must eliminate your reactions to the noise and follow the signal.

Take "Fast Market" or Climax Condition Profits

In day trading it's a good idea to exit a profitable trade if the market climaxes on heavy volume or "fast market" conditions. There's a high probability that the high or low of the day is being made at this time. If the market hits your resting entry orders under these conditions, expect immediate profits or be alert for another wave in the same direction.

Abandon Dull or Nonperforming Stocks

If you find yourself in a stock that is very quiet, look elsewhere. Time is scarce and watching a dull stock drains energy.

SETUPS

There are three categories of setups that warrant explanation.

1. Market setup
2. Computer setup
3. Chart setup

Market Setup

The first setup stems from the natural rhythm of the market. George Douglass Taylor, in *The Taylor Trading Technique* (Trader's Press, 1994), describes this rhythm in terms of three-day to five-day swings in the market. A swing low day followed by a sell day might mean an extension of the previous day and then a sell-short day that would lead to the next buy day. Provisions should be made for a strong or weak stock that might extend the number of days in the swing to five. An example of this can be seen in Figure 13.1. Understanding where the market is in the swing helps you formulate a plan for any particular day.

Computer Setup

For our short-term trading we use just four proprietary computer-generated numbers (see Figure 13.2):

1. Short-term trend identifier
2. Long-term trend identifier
3. Short-term momentum oscillator
4. Long-term momentum oscillator

This category can include any number of commonly used or esoteric computer-generated numbers that you feel comfortable using. One common error, in my view, that many traders make is to rely on this tool to the exclusion of either the stock setup or our next category, chart setup.

FIGURE 13.1   Three- to Five-Day Swings

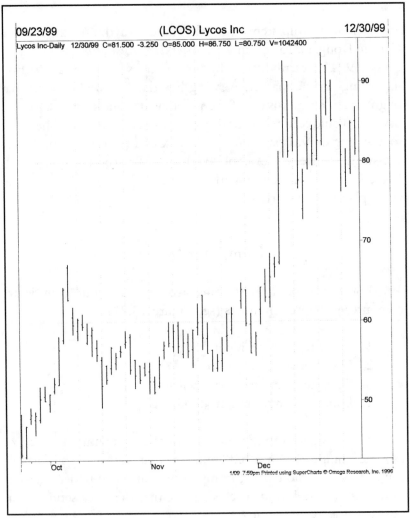

Chart Setup

Here I focus on using charting techniques that can stand alone or be used in conjunction with our other setup categories. They include:

FIGURE 13.2 Computer-Generated Numbers

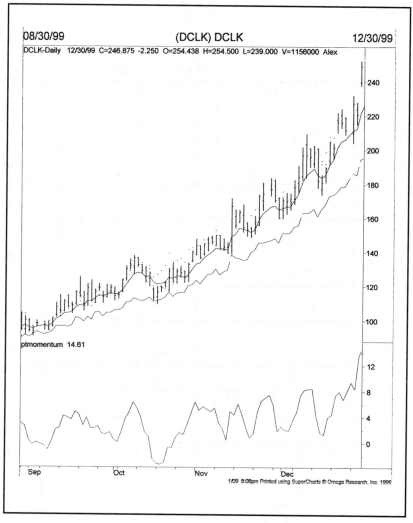

- Natural market retracements
- Trendlines and pattern recognition
- Daily or two-day patterns
- Highs and lows

As you review each chart in relationship to its set-up category, keep in mind that actual trading occurs on the hard right edge of the chart not yet formed. Being mentally tough involves identifying opportunity and then acting accordingly.

Natural market retracements. Market retracements include Fibonacci ratios, Gann Fan lines, Elliot Wave, and the like. Figure 13.3 is an example of Amgen's finding support at the 50 percent

FIGURE 13.3   Fibonacci .682 and .50 Retracement

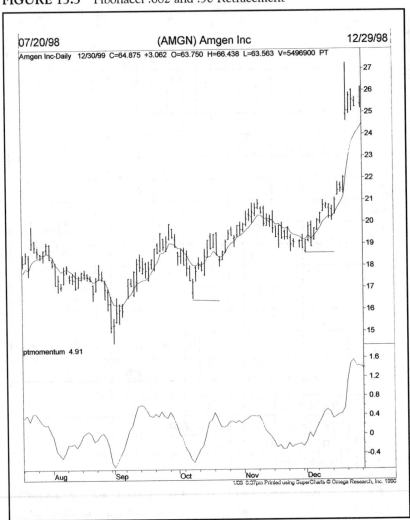

retracement level and Figure 13.4 is an example of Gann Fan lines. Also included in this setup category are market retracements to moving averages. The setup of market retracements is usually most effective when the market tests these areas on buy days or sell-short days in the natural swing.

FIGURE 13.4 Gann Fan Lines

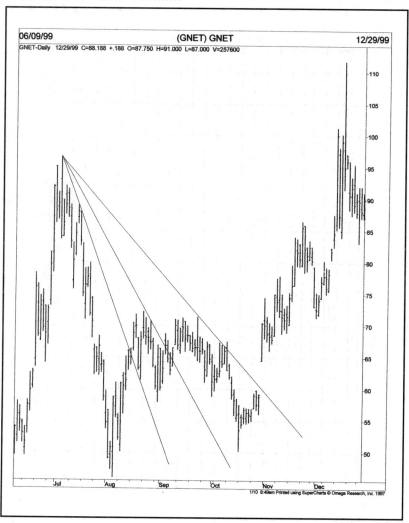

171

Trendlines and pattern recognition. Many times the simplest devices are the most effective, as we can see in Figure 13.5. The bottom triangle breakout leads to a flag pattern consolidation with increasing volatility and opportunity. The flags and pennant patterns are textbook. Traders may either buy the small pullbacks in the flag

FIGURE 13.5   Flag and Triangle Patterns

pattern or wait for the breakout and follow the market strength or weakness.

Daily or two-day patterns. These patterns include the following (see Figure 13.6):

1. *An outside day (OD)* is one in which the day's range is above and below that of the previous day's range. The day following an outside day can usually be traded by buying dips and selling rallies.

2. *An inside day (ID)* is one in which the day's range is below the high and above the low of the previous day's range. Inside days are often followed by increased volatility and should be traded by buying the breakout above the previous day's high and selling a breakout below the previous day's low.

3. *A constricted-range day (CRD)* is one in which the range contracts to the smallest range of the past several days. Sometimes the stock will contract over two or more days. Patience here can provide opportunity. This is another pattern where the trader should be prepared to trade the breakouts in either direction.

4. *A wide-range day (WRD)* refers to a range that is considerably larger than the past several days. Wide-range days are usually followed by trading-range days, and the trader should look to buy breaks and sell rallies.

5. *Two-day highs and lows* indicate markets that tend to test the previous day's high or low and can provide the lowest-risk trades available. When the trader can combine these tests with either a computer-generated number setup or a chart setup, it becomes a very low-risk, potentially high-reward, trade.

FIGURE 13.6 Daily Patterns

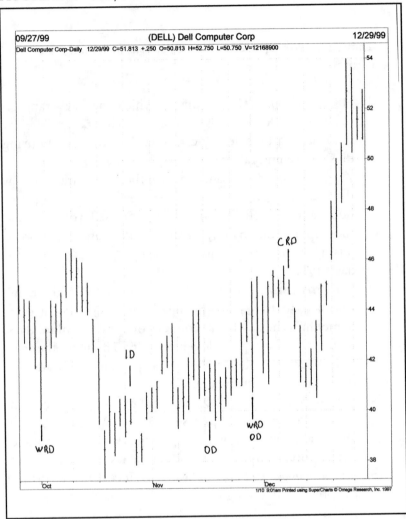

CREATING A ROAD MAP
FOR TRADES

Consistency in planning is as important as consistency in execution. Preparation and planning to be able to anticipate market action can only be effective if the trader is consistent with the various elements of his or her methodology.

Landmarks on the road map to a trade are:

- Trend
- Swing location of the market
- Pattern recognition
- One-day or two-day bar patterns
- Computer-generated numbers

Trend

The first step is to identify the stock's trend. My habit is to use simple daily bar charts with my computer-generated numbers superimposed onto the chart. Some traders are more numbers-oriented and need merely to look at a set of numbers to fix the market in their mind. Although I enjoy modern technology, I have continued to update daily charts because it reinforces a sense of continuity for each stock even though there may not have been any trade opportunities.

The important point is that the trader must determine in his or her mind if a particular market is in an uptrend, downtrend, or sideways trend. Simple trendlines or higher highs and higher lows, and lower highs and lower lows, will establish a trend. I have also included my proprietary computer-generated numbers on my charts because they have a strong reliability for anticipating support and resistance areas of the market. (See Figure 13.7.) As you can see in Figure 13.8, Apple Computer was well into an uptrend when it retraced and traded on the long-term trend ID area. This creates low-risk opportunities for swing traders. The operative word here is *low* risk, not *no* risk; traders who are looking for the latter will forever be complaining about the markets that got away.

Another example of the use of trend identification is shown is Figure 13.9. This chart shows an uptrend and Fibonacci retracement numbers superimposed on it. As you can see, anticipating a retrace-

FIGURE 13.7 Trend Identification

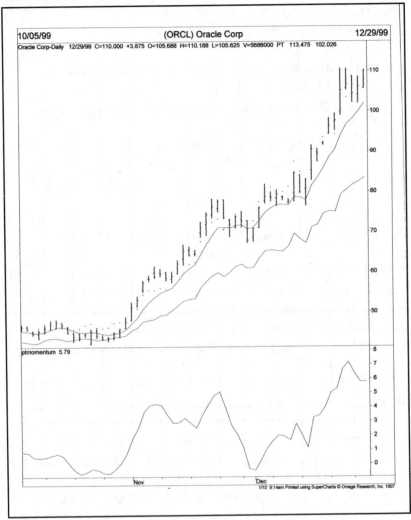

ment test of either .384 or .50 of the uptrend put you in position to make very low-risk trades with large potential. In later sections we see how swing analysis and daily bar patterns help to trade this market on a swing trade basis. However, notice how the market makes it to the full .50 correction. Realistically, no one can know

FIGURE 13.8   Trend Identification

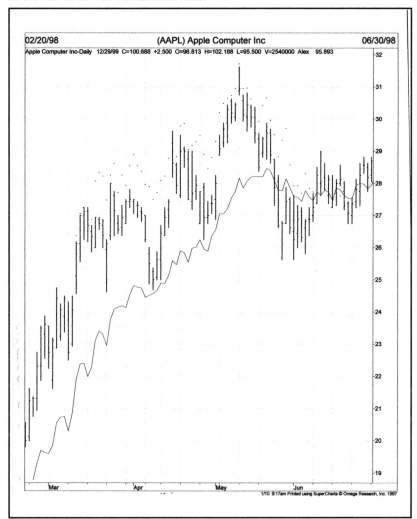

whether this stock goes up or down from this correction point, but we have found a high probability setup and that is all one can ask for. The point is not the specific methods shown in this section on trend identification. Rather, it is that whatever method you feel comfortable using should be the first thing on your daily agenda.

177

FIGURE 13.9   Fibonacci Retracement in Uptrend

Swing Location of the Market

Determining where a market is in its three-day to five-day swing pattern will go a long way to improving profitability. In *The Taylor Trading Technique* (Traders Press, 1994), George Taylor breaks down the market to a "buy day," a "sell day," and a "sell-short day." Once

178

this rhythm is established, the trader should also pay attention to how and when the lows and highs are made each day. For example, buy days should have lows made first and sell-short days should have highs made first. For the most part, experienced traders have always sensed that morning lows in a market are a low-risk buy area. The old adage of buying a lower opening in a bull market and selling a higher opening in a bear market is still a viable operating procedure. And it is also very important for day traders as well. Morning weakness into support has a good potential to react profitably as the day wears on. However, most afternoon breaks into support are not as reliable. The same, of course, goes for morning strength into resistance. So, as swing traders we should be aware of the swing location setup as well as the daily setup to maximize our profit potential.

Pattern Recognition

Sometimes the most important landmarks are the simplest concepts. Trendlines that define several days of highs or lows create tests that are low-risk opportunities. (See Figure 13.10.) The buy day bar (B) was followed by a sell day rally to the trendline, and the next day, which was a sell-short day, never violated that trendline. In Figure 13.11 we see an example of a triangle pattern and the breakout of that pattern for a day trade. You can see that the triangle formation ends with three constricted-range days in a row setting up the volatile move. Breakout moves or gap openings, although difficult to enter, often yield large payoffs. Many times the wider the gap opening, the stronger the move in that direction. Although there is a danger of a false breakout, a reversal of this kind of pattern should be followed because of its reliability.

One-Day or Two-Day Bar Patterns

Only a limited number of possible patterns can take place in the previous day or two, but they offer us some of the best opportunities for the lowest-risk, high-probability trades. Markets seem to

FIGURE 13.10 Market Swing

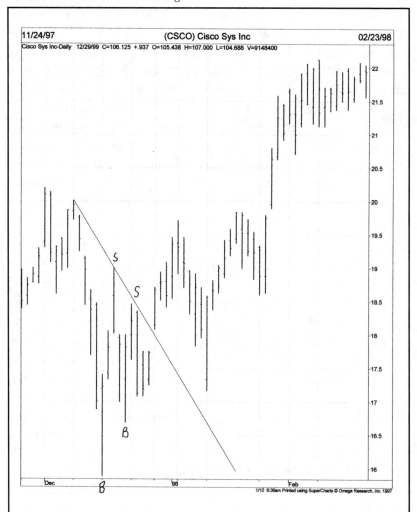

constantly test the previous day's high or low, and we should come
to expect these tests. (See Figure 13.12.) A strong stock usually
makes a higher low, while some markets take out the previous low
and snap back as evidence of probable support. If a market trades
under the lows and finds no support, get out. We can also see in

FIGURE 13.11   Triangle Pattern

Figure 13.13 that the first two tests marked with "Xs" were buy days or tests of buy day lows, and the third bar marked with an "X" is a sell day and a test of the previous day's high. Combining the swing rhythm with the two-day pattern can put you on the right side of the day's movement and offers the most logical entry point.

FIGURE 13.12   Two-Day Patterns

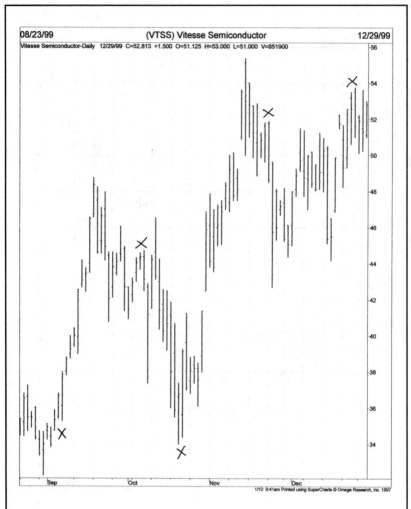

The outside days shown in Figure 13.13, which close on the ranges' extremes, usually have some follow through that can be faded for a day trade. An outside day that does not close at the extreme of its range usually is followed by an inside day. As the mar-

FIGURE 13.13   Outside Days

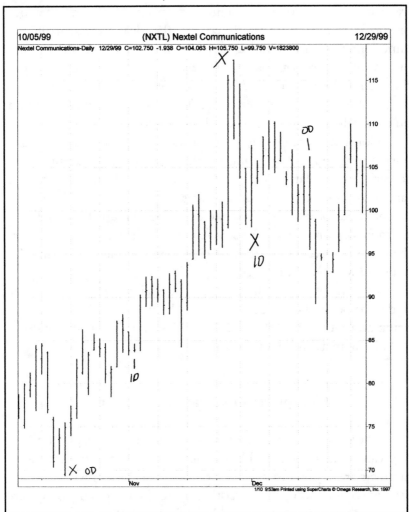

ket wizard Linda Bradford Raschke put it, "The market seems to use up all its bullets in one day."

Inside days are not interesting in themselves but for what they can produce in opportunity. Expanded ranges often follow inside days as seen in Figure 13.13. An ID usually indicates a breakout trade and requires some preparation and planning. Several breakout or volatility systems are published, but the ideas are essentially the same. Enter at some distance from either the close or open, or high or low, of the previous bar or of the second previous bar. I believe the high and low of the previous day works well, and, if there is a failure of the move, gives the trader the opportunity to turn around on the trade with a reasonable risk parameter.

Constricted-range days—either one or several in a row—also portend expanded ranges and breakout trades. The extent of the constriction is relative to the ranges over several recent days. The same methodology for breakout trades used above for the inside day can be used for constricted-range days. (See Figure 13.14.) There are more occurrences of whipsaw action, but the narrow ranges keep the losses so circumscribed that turning on the trade and going the opposite way is a sound tactic.

I've mentioned expanded ranges several times and it's nice for traders to be on the right side of them. However, we have seen that being aware of them offers opportunities on subsequent days so I include them as an important category.

Computer-Generated Numbers

There are no magic numbers—and certainly no magic numbers that can stand alone as a full trading system. Computer-generated numbers are a tool, just as are other tools discussed previously to be used in conjunction with each other. I use three types of computer-generated numbers that are calculated for two different time frames: the trend identifiers, an oscillator, and the pivots which are derived from the oscillator. (See Figure 13.15.)

The pivot numbers are the prices the stock must continue to exceed in order to maintain the current slope of the oscillator. When the pivot moves from above to below the market, or vice versa, the market's range tends to expand and should be traded in that direc-

FIGURE 13.14   Constricted-Range Days

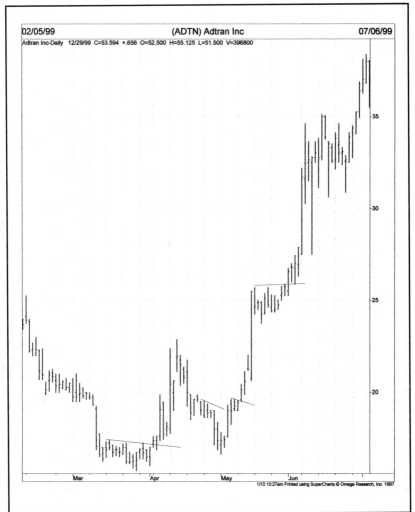

tion. The pivots are also reliable price points for support and resistance on a daily basis.

As a market's trend flattens out, it will trade between the intermediate-term trend price and the intermediate-term pivot. This will define the sideways trend that develops either as a contin-

FIGURE 13.15 Computer-Generated Numbers

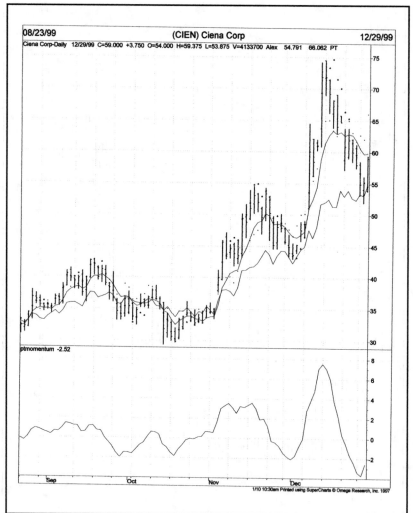

uation pattern, a bottom, or a top. (See Figure 13.15.) While this
is taking place, the short-term pivot and either of the intermediate-
term prices become support and resistance areas and many times
define the days' ranges. (See Figure 13.15.)

The short-term oscillator on the bottom of Figure 13.15 is a very useful tool. It has definite overbought and oversold areas that allow taking advantage of the pivot movement and either exit a current position or take a new one at or near tops and bottoms of market swings.

Many useful computer-generated systems are available, such as ADX, MACD, Stocastics, RSI, and Bollinger Bands, among others. It is a mistake, however, to isolate these devices and trade only on their single input.

Each trader must find the tools that are comfortable for her or him and blend them into a methodology that fits one's personality. The computer numbers I use have been traded day-in and day-out for more than 15 years. During this time they have been refined, tested, and retested to ensure their reliability in different market conditions. That is where my market confidence comes from. Having said all this, I still realize they're only numbers! Mental toughness is trading with confidence based on well researched ideas with a statistically reliable track record.

14

Moving from One Winning Stock Trade to Another

I've discussed all the landmarks on the road map to successful trading, but we can't reach our destination if we don't plan our trip and make the trade. No serious traveler goes on a journey without taking out a map and thinking through the various alternatives, obstacles, and scenarios that the trip might entail. It's the same with trading!

Through hundreds of interviews, close personal relationships with some of the country's best traders, and my personal market experience, I have never met a consistently profitable trader who hasn't prepared rigorously for trading. The most important part of your preparation must be preparing yourself emotionally, that is, psychologically and physically, to be resourceful, disciplined, and committed to whatever the market throws your way.

Remember, it all comes down to these three things:

1. Identifying an opportunity
2. Taking action automatically
3. Feeling good about the trade—knowing you did the right thing whether that particular trade is profitable or not

Identifying an Opportunity

It's decision time. You have all these tools with which to identify one or more opportunities, based on probability. You have found the swing location, or a double bottom or top setup, or an inside day setup for a possible breakout. Write them down and be prepared to act!

Taking Action Automatically

You must be resolved, disciplined, and consistent in acting on your ideas and performing the necessary hard work. Every day that the market behaves as you have anticipated will reinforce your discipline and confidence.

Feeling Good about the Trade

Each trade you have made following the format outlined here is a good trade whether it turns a profit or a loss. Trading is a process and the result at the end of the process is the important thing, not each small element (individual trade) of that process. Your small losses are just operating costs that you have made to generate business. You must truly believe this and operate from this trading attitude.

The following setups and trading patterns are day trading opportunities common to the trading floor and to off-floor trading in every market. I would now like to expand upon, through illustrations and discussion, the trading ideas that I mentioned earlier. Additional examples of tests discussed previously are shown in Figure 14.1 and Figure 14.2.

Figure 14.3 shows a new high breakout of a month-long consolidation. The powerful element of this setup is the constricted-range day that precedes the breakout to new highs. Combining a breakout trade with a new high allows us to trail a very close stop as this trade should not violate the CRD low.

FIGURE 14.1   Additional Examples of Tests

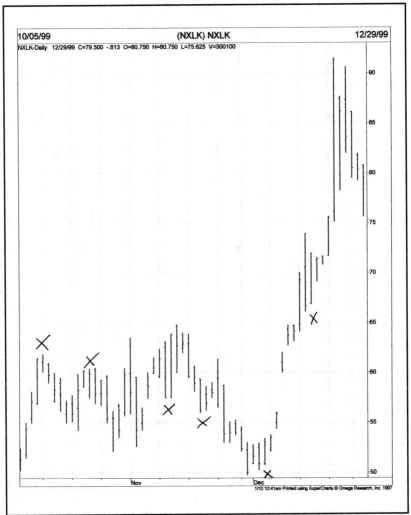

In Figure 14.3 the only difference is that the CRD breakout occurs after a short consolidation pattern just above the new high breakout.

Figure 14.3 shows a CRD/ID one day after a new high breakout, and this precedes a very reliable trade the next day. This market

FIGURE 14.2   Bottom Test

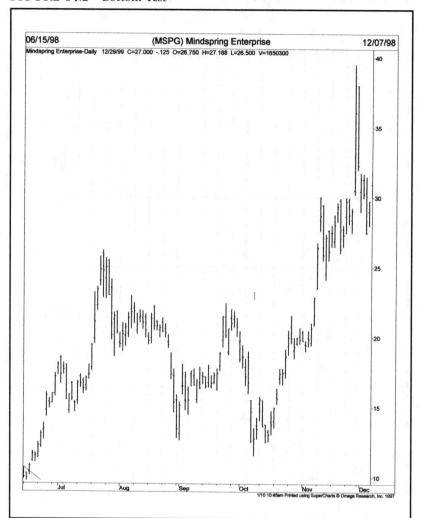

06/15/98   (MSPG) Mindspring Enterprise   12/07/98

Mindspring Enterprise-Daily   12/29/99 C=27.000 -.125 O=26.750 H=27.188 L=26.500 V=1650300

should not trade below the ID low. Figure 14.4 is another example of an ID preceding a breakout.

The use of the breakout day, such as a CRD and ID in conjunction with other patterns, can be further seen in Figure 14.5 at the double bottom that was formed in Novellus. Because we can't

FIGURE 14.3   New High Breakout

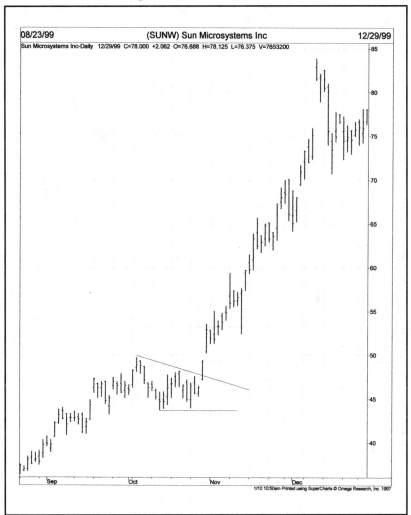

know if the double bottom is completed, we can use the ID as the trigger to enter the market, and the low of the move can be our stop.

If a stock is testing a previous bottom made at least five days before, then buy the stock one tick higher than the high made on the day of the test. This is illustrated in Figure 14.5.

FIGURE 14.4 Double Bottom with ID

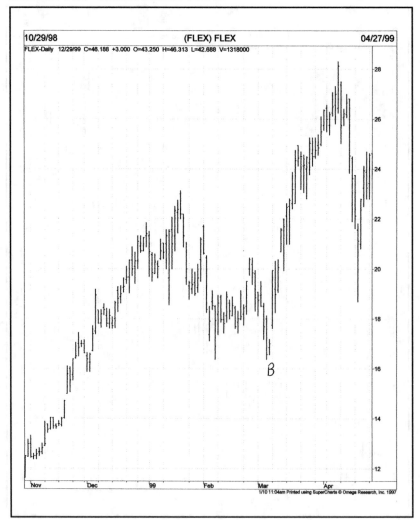

Tops are very similar, and the trader can use this pattern to sell longs or to initiate a short position with little risk. For tops you should enter your sell orders one tick below the low of the day on which the price tested the high. (See Figure 14.6.)

FIGURE 14.5   Double Bottom Next-Day Buy

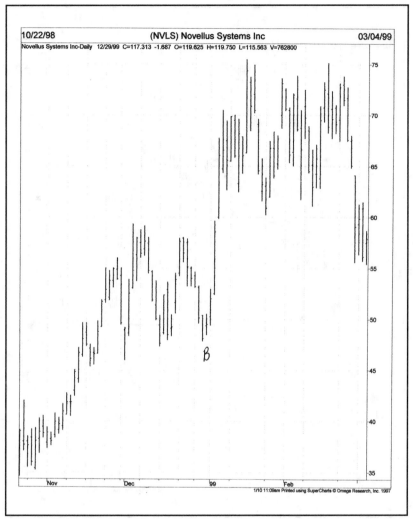

I spoke about buying or selling on or against trendlines or moving averages. Each trader should develop a method to help him or her enter and exit the market. Two approaches that I have seen used successfully are buying or selling directly on the trendline or

FIGURE 14.6 Double Top Next-Day Sell

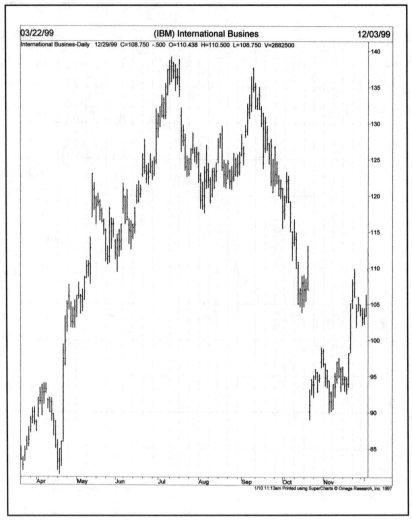

moving average, and exiting if the stock closes below the buy or above the sell point, and buying or selling the next day above or below the previous day's range. (See Figure 14.7 and Figure 14.8.) Trendlines and moving averages do not in themselves compose a

FIGURE 14.7   Using a Moving Average

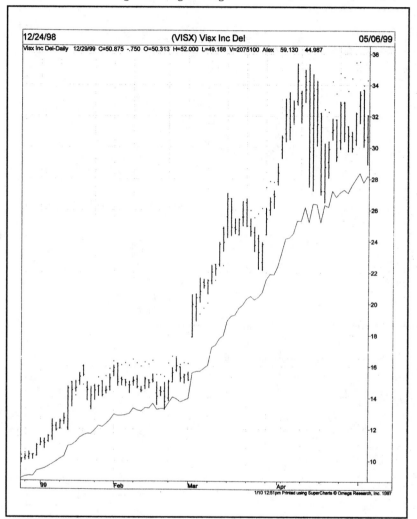

system, but they are very effective tools to use with other decision-making devices.

Sometimes a failed trade is the best information your money can buy. One of my favorite tactics is to buy or sell a failed break-

FIGURE 14.8 Using a Trendline

down or breakout. If the stock closes below the moving average or trendline and snaps back above the moving average or trendline within two days, a very strong probability of more movement in that direction is indicated. (See Figure 14.9.)

FIGURE 14.9 Buying the Snap Back

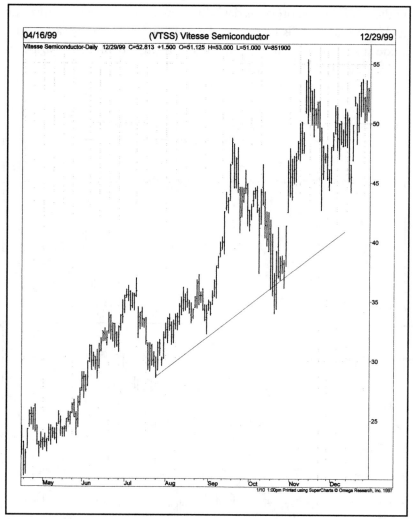

One of the more powerful ideas already mentioned deserves more attention: the two-day test, especially on the second or third day of a swing. Most stocks trade with a rhythm of their own. In an uptrend or downtrend, a swing may extend for three, four, or five days before losing its momentum. Many times a stock will open higher and test the previous day's high by trading close to or through it. If the market falls back into the previous day's range, a low-risk trade is set up by selling the stock and using the high as a stop loss point. (See Figure 14.10.)

FIGURE 14.10   The Two-Day Test

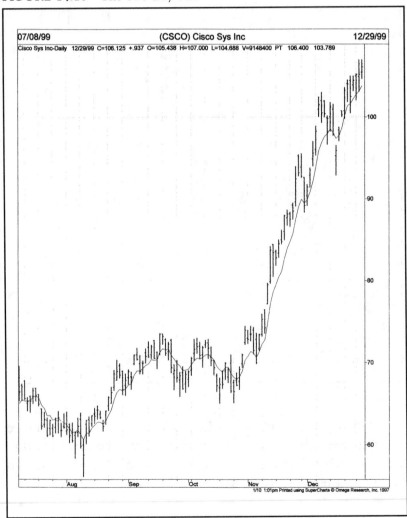

The mistake many traders make is not entering markets advantageously, at junctures of circumscribed risk, thus producing feelings of psychological confusion, ambiguity, or hesitation.

In Part Four, I will synthesize the technical concepts discussed here with a discussion and summary of the preparation and commitment required to be a mentally tough online trader, whether your trading time horizon is long term or that of the active short-term trader.

PART 4

The Successful
Online Trader

15

Becoming a Mentally Tough Trader: Competing on a Level Playing Field

The technological playing field is now level. If you are operating on a Nasdaq Level 1 or Level 2 screen, you have at your fingertips information that a short time ago was only available to market professionals. You can instantly access real-time quotes, depth of market, and technical indicators. If you want fundamental information, a click of the mouse gives you rank, beta, price-earnings ratios, 52-week highs and lows, dividend rates, earnings estimates, and more. But the real key to competing favorably, as we have seen, is committing to become a mentally tough online trader and mastering the internal strategies necessary to overcome the psychological setbacks that the market is so good at instigating in all of us.

Top traders have taught themselves how to become mentally tough as well as psychologically resilient to the subjective demands exerted on themselves by the market. James Loehr recommends the following regime for world-class athletes to maintain mental toughness. Its applicability for traders is obvious.

- *Always play with intensity.* Generating, managing, and controlling intensity is a skill to be learned and practiced.

- *When pressure mounts, get more aggressive.* The common response to high pressure situations is to become conservative. Loehr, however, notes the strategy of hoping that or waiting for your opponent to make an error is a dead-end strategy. For traders, the typical response to a losing position or trade is to "wait and see," rather than to aggressively go with the market. The top traders play to win; they don't play not to lose. Of course, there is always an assumption, notwithstanding one's level of intensity of aggressiveness of strictly calculated risk management, given their unique market perspective (e.g., long term, swing, or day).
- *Love the battle.* Enjoy the trading process. (Yes, it is possible.)
- *Crises and adversity are the real tests of mental toughness.* The mental edge in trading, as in sports, is the realization that when things get tough you feel challenged.
- *Leave mistakes behind.* Look ahead and proceed with a positive expectation.
- *Project a great image.* If you project a image of confidence, energy, determination, and control, what you show on the outside is the way you will come to feel on the inside.
- *Use humor to break tension.* Loehr writes, "The rule of thumb is this: if you can maintain your sense of humor, you're in control." Humor provides perspective, fun, and control to difficult situations on the playing field and in the stock market.
- *Never run out of options.* The goal for the trader, as well as the athlete, is never to run out of options. "You're always probing for a weakness that will give you a new foothold, a creative answer to a stubborn problem." For the trader, mental toughness is the result of always being engaged, experiencing the winner's state of mind. The list below reveals the key characteristics of the winner's state of mind.
  - *Establish a personal standard of excellence.*
  - *Create an internal environment for success.*
  - *Expect the best of yourself.*
  - *Know yourself.*

THE WINNER'S STATE OF MIND

Establish a Personal Standard of Excellence

Knute Rockne used to say, "Show me a good loser and I'll show you a loser." Successful trading is all about winning—internal and external. The key to successful trading, as we have seen, is to feel like a winner even though you may be temporarily losing, representing that loss as part of an overall process of gaining confidence and competence.

Establishing a personal standard of excellence is a minimum standard. The top traders have all learned this. They constantly read and study and refine their techniques. They do what is necessary to consistently win. As one top trader put it, "I try to improve my trading by 1 percent every day. At the end of the year, this is a staggering number."

Understanding your motives and establishing concrete goals will allow you to maintain a consistently high standard of performance. By defining exactly what steps are necessary to secure your goals, you can routinely adopt appropriate actions. As Thomas Huxley observed, "The great end [goal] of life is not knowledge but action." Adopting a standard of excellence will permit you to achieve your trading goals and experience the success you are capable of attaining. Grant Tinker, the television producer, said, "First we will be best, and then we will be first." This philosophy applies as much to trading as it does to getting top television ratings. Hard work and discipline and belief all combine to establish the standard that will guarantee ultimate success.

Create an Internal Environment for Success

In order to be successful as a trader you must create an atmosphere that is pleasant and comfortable, where your trading can flourish. You must also create a positive psychological dialogue with yourself based on the empowering imagery of a visual, auditory, and kinesthetic nature. This will result in a high level of self-confidence and focused concentration. Trading will also be experienced as effortless, highly enjoyable, and in control. The formula for creating a successful internal dialogue is to create imagery that respects you; that makes you feel important. Don't criticize, condemn, or complain. "Kvetching" and moaning won't help.

Keep your ego out of trading. Concentrate on how you can develop as a trader, how you can increase your base of knowledge and improve your execution strategies. This involves working to constantly improve. Work for excellence, not perfection. Again, remember excellence provides results, perfection produces ulcers!

Concentrate on solutions. Don't reiterate problems. Identify your own strengths and weaknesses. Learn from your mistakes. Also take personal responsibility for *all* decisions, not just the good trades!

Invest your time wisely. Concentrate on what works. It is essential that you direct your focus on the practical and not solely on the theoretical. And most importantly, always keep in mind there is a tomorrow. Don't try to do it all today!

Communicating Effectively with Yourself

When I conduct trading seminars I always offer the mnemonic TORCH FIRE to represent the essential ingredients in communicating effectively with oneself. The key elements are listed below.

- *Trust.* Learn to trust yourself. Follow your instincts—you will be pleasantly surprised.
- *Open.* Be open-minded.
- *Respect.* Respect yourself by not speaking harshly to yourself. Stay positive.
- *Challenge.* Set goals and challenges for yourself that are realistic and will help to build confidence.

- *Humor.* Have a sense of humor. Remember trading is a process; it can be a lot of fun.
- *Faith.* Have ultimate faith (belief) in yourself and your proven methodology.
- *Interested.* Keep you interest level high by constantly improving.
- *Results.* Be results oriented.
- *Enthusiasm.* Be in the right state of mind—enthusiastic and energized.

Communicating effectively with yourself will bring out your ability and allow you to succeed by making the right trading decisions. Ralph Waldo Emerson observed: "Your mind is a sacred enclosure into which nothing harmful can enter except by your permission."

Expect the Best of Yourself

As I have already stated, many traders, in a psychological sense, don't trade to win. They trade not to lose! When you trade not to lose you can never achieve peak performance. In order to derive the best of yourself, you must take defined risk: you must take decisive and automatic action and do everything in your power to win. Expecting the best of yourself at all times will allow you to create and maintain a resourceful psychological state, regardless of trading circumstances or conditions.

The real test, of course, is not when things are going great for you, but rather, when things get tough, the pressure is high, and the trading seems to be spinning out of control. At these times it is essential to expect the best of yourself based on your commitment, hard work, and discipline. In other words, confidence based on competence will allow you to stay relaxed, focused, concentrated, highly motivated, and most importantly, in control.

I'm reminded of a story I once heard about Arthur Rubinstein, the famous pianist. When Rubinstein was in his nineties he was asked if his hands ever hurt when he played. Rubinstein thought for a moment and then answered, "Only when I hit the wrong notes!" When times are difficult, that is the true test of how successful you are in applying good psychological skills. The literature is ripe with a wealth of psychological studies that report the importance of positive perception on performance. How you perceive yourself will ultimately determine your outcome. Trading constantly presents us with obstacles and opportunities. Expecting the best of yourself is the best means for dealing constructively with both of them.

Know Yourself

There is an ancient Talmudic expression that states, "to change and to improve are two vastly different things." In order to improve at trading or anything else, you must begin by knowing yourself, learning what are the things that motivate your actions. What role do fear, doubt, and worry play in your life? How important is it for you to be successful? The more you understand about yourself, the more effective you will be at trading and everything else. By learning what your current trading motives are, you can establish goals and a system of beliefs that will assure success. By directing your focus and by conditioning yourself to have an ongoing positive internal dialogue in terms of your specific beliefs, feelings, and imagery, you can choose how you, as an individual, internally represent external market phenomena. You are free to improve yourself as much as you like.

Go as far as you can see, and when you get there, you will see further.—Anonymous

Some people have trouble improving because they identify with failure and hardship. The mentally tough online traders choose to self-identify with winning and ease through practice.

Those who identify with the Tao are likewise welcomed by the Tao.—Tao Te Ching

Responsibility

Taking responsibility for whatever happens in the market is an obvious point, but traders often find it difficult to internalize it. In *The New Market Wizards* (Harper, 1992), Jack Schwager writes, "Understand that you are responsible for your own results. Even if you lost on your broker's tips, an advisory service's recommendations, or a bad signal from the system you bought, you are responsible because you made the decision to listen and act." A trader who blames others for bad outcomes will never be successful. Schwager, who interviewed dozens of Wall Street's and Chicago's most successful traders, concluded that the methods employed by exceptional traders are extraordinarily diverse. Some were pure fundamentalists, other employed only technical analysis, and still others combined both approaches. Still, specific commonalties were abundantly clear. For the sake of summary, the key points to remember are:

- Be sure that you want to trade. It is common for people who think they want to trade to discover that they really don't.
- Establish a personal standard of excellence.
- Examine your motives for trading.
- Match your investment method to your personality.
- Use both halves of your brain: learn to trust your intuition.
- It is absolutely necessary to have an edge.
- The type of method is not important, but having one is critical.
- Developing a method is hard work. Shortcuts rarely lead to trading success.
- Have trading goals that are precise, realistic, and measurable.
- Good trading should be effortless, automatic, and decisive in its implementation.
- Good money management and risk control are essential. Never risk more than 1 to 2 percent of your capital on any trade. Predetermine your exit point before you get into a trade. Cut trading size down sharply during losing periods.
- If you lose a predetermined amount of your initial capital, stop trading until you regain confidence in your trading.

- You must have an investment plan.
- Discipline is key in all phases of the investment process.
- Independence of thought and action is critical. The trader must be able to make his or her own trading decisions.
- Confidence based on competence is essential.
- Loss is not accidental, it is inevitable.
- Trade only when you feel confident and optimistic.
- Don't rely on tips or the advice of others.
- Patience is your edge. Waiting for the right setup or high probability trade greatly increases your chance for a successful result.
- It is important to learn how to sit with profits if you have a particular exit target.
- Alter position size according to market conditions and volatility.
- Consistency in trading is more important than just being right. Methodological consistency based on research is the key to success.
- Don't trade to please others.
- You do not need to capture an entire trend. Catching just part of a market move is just fine.
- Never have loyalty to a position that is going against you.
- Don't be afraid to take partial profits. Learn how to scale in and out of trades.
- Hope is a symptom of a losing trade.
- You won't win if you are trading on short money. You can't trade on a shoestring.
- When the market lets you off the hook too easily, it is often an indication of a winning position.
- Stay focused and open-minded.
- If you are looking for excitement, don't trade. The calm state of mind of the trader is essential for trading success.
- Top traders know how to identify and eliminate anxiety in their trading.
- Pay attention to intuition.

Jeff Jensen, a successful online trader, characterizes his trading approach this way:

> I've started adopting more of a hedge mentality. Instead of scalping intra-day positions, I'm doing swing trading, holding the positions; always trying to buy quality companies. My decisions are based on research: buying these issues at good entry levels after price pull backs; loading up on a break for a couple of day moves after a sell-off.

With a bias always to the long side of the market, he looks to hedge his position against competing names within a sector. Jensen explains his market actions as follows:

> My bias is to the long side of the market. But what I'll do is hedge my position with some shorts. I'll look at a competitor name or select a similar company in the sector of the stock that I'm bullish about and use a short sale for protection. The idea being that if there's some bad sector news, I'm protected by the short sale.
>
> You need to learn when you're most vulnerable psychologically.
>
> When you're in a long position you've got this trade going for you, you're hopeful and excited. It's profitable and you keep thinking it's just going to keep rallying. And at that time is when you usually need to take profit. And when you're in a long position and it's going against you, but it's within support, you need to be confident that your analysis is still valid, which means you don't bail out. I will usually even buy more or be a buyer in similar stocks . . . It's just hard to manage your emotions when you're in a position. So you need to work on this part of trading. It is critical.
>
> Many times I'm just talking to myself. If you've missed the move long or short, you can't chase the market. And a lot of times you want to chase it or if you miss the long move you'll try to short it. It can be crazy! You just need to sit back

and realize the market will be here tomorrow. There's always going to be another opportunity if you approach trading with pragmatism and discipline.

Mariano Mendoza is also a successful online trader who only trades small cap stocks. He attributes his success to following his own path: being mentally tough and well disciplined in his market approach. He explains:

It took a year before I came around to what I'm using now, identifying small cap stocks that are poised for breakout moves. The first year I bobbed around doing a lot of different things: listening to other traders, trading big caps—following all the advice that ended up not working! Finally I decided I was adopting the wrong path and I just quit listening to all the advice and did something different and it worked!

I constantly look at price charts. I am continuously typing in names on a ticker. I am searching the charts for familiar patterns that I know from experience are ready for breakouts. It is important to trust yourself and your method. This is the emotional part. Forcing yourself to do what you believe is the right thing. I mean, you need the support of a system or consistent methodology. First of all, you have to set up a system! But, that's not even the hardest thing. Once you have set up a system, you have to prove to yourself that it's right. And you need to be psychologically prepared to follow its rules. Most traders set rules for themselves and every day they'll break them. You'll set a rule, like I won't get out until support is violated—sounds simple right? In the end that's the difference between success and failure.

NEW WORLD OF TRADING

It is a brave new world for consumers when it comes to investing and financial services. Online brokers and financial services companies have opened the door to an unprecedented degree of consumer financial self-management. The need for investor education has never been greater, due in large part to the convenience and easy access that is provided by online trading. In 1999, Securities and Exchange Commission chairman Arthur Levitt stated:

> Over the past two years, particularly in recent months, the SEC has been hearing concerns about retail, online [Internet] investing. In fact, the number of complaints concerning online investing has increased by 330 percent in the last year. Some of the issues raised specifically relate to online trading, others are generic to all investing. The majority of them can be addressed through better education and investors ensuring that they have done their homework.

It is clear that the government is closely monitoring online investing. Attorney General of the State of New York, Eliot Spitzer, conducted a nine-month investigation into the online trading industry, which has resulted in a cooperative effort between Spitzer and the Securities Industry Association (SIA) to fund a public awareness campaign. In a press release issued November 22, 1999, Spitzer stated:

> With this new technology comes the need for new 'rules of the road' for both investors and brokerage firms. As we're constantly finding, the information superhighway can be filled with potholes for the unsuspecting, unprepared or uninformed.

The findings of his study conclude with this advice to consumers:

> Making sound investment decisions requires much more than the click of a mouse; nothing can substitute for good old-fashioned research and education.
>
> My office will continue to work with and monitor the industry to ensure that investors are adequately informed and protected. By doing so, we hope to smooth out as many

rough spots as possible on this section of the information superhighway.

The keys to being a mentally tough online trader are simply stated, but again, not easily achieved.

- Do your research; be an informed and educated investor.
- Learn a proven trading methodology that is adaptable to a variety of market conditions.
- Learn how to take a loss.
- Internalize the psychological skills of winning.
- Learn the essential elements of a successful trading strategy.
- Invest time and resources in ongoing education.

The Big Picture

There is an old Hindu legend that at one time all men on earth were gods, but men so sinned and abused the Divine that Brahma, the god of all gods, decided that the godhead should be taken away from man and hidden someplace where he would never find it again to abuse it.

One god said, "Let's bury it deep in the earth."

Brahma said, "No, man will learn to excavate and find it there someday."

Another god said, "Then let's put it in the deepest sea."

Brahma said, "No, man will learn to descend to the bottom and find it there, too."

A third god suggested, "Why don't we hide it on the highest mountain?"

Brahma said, "No, man will climb the highest mountain. I have a better place! Let's hide it down in man himself. He will never think to look there."

Within each of us is the power to accomplish what we want in trading and everything else if we just stop looking outside ourselves for easy answers. There are no magic bullets in trading and investing. No Holy Grail. No secret elixirs. Many time-tested investment strategies, when applied properly, will work. The key resides always in the development and fulfillment of our own personal characteristics and attitudes: confidence, judgement, courage, fortitude, intellect, prudence, and commitment.

We have once again come full circle, as traders and as human beings. The uncertain is always confronting us anew with spectacular challenges in a 360-degree universe of possibilities. The choice is ours to seize or shrink from opportunity. Success requires nothing less than mental toughness and level-headed judgment based on an ongoing commitment to self-mastery.

Now focus.

For Further Reading

Abell, Howard. *The Day Trader's Advantage: How to Move from One Winning Position to the Next.* Chicago: Dearborn, 1997.

Abell, Howard. *Digital Day Trading: How to Move from One Winning Stock Position to the Next.* Chicago: Dearborn, 1999.

Abell Howard. *Risk Reward.* Chicago: Dearborn, 1998.

Abell, Howard. *Spread Trading.* Chicago: Dearborn, 1998.

Abell, Howard. *The Electronic Trading of Options.* Chicago: Dearborn, 1999.

Abell, Howard and Koppel, Robert. *The Market Savvy Investor.* Chicago: Dearborn, 1999.

Barach, Roland. *Mindtraps: Mastering the Inner World of Investing.* Homewood: Dow Jones-Irwin, 1988.

Baruch, Bernard M. *Baruch: My Own Story.* New York: Holt, Rinehart and Winston, 1957.

Davis, Rod. *What You Need to Know before You Invest.* New York: Barron's, 1999.

Douglas, Mark. *The Disciplined Trader.* New York: New York Institute of Finance, 1990.

Eng, William F. *The Day Trader's Manual: Theory Art, and Science of Profitable Short-Term Investing.* New York: John Wiley, 1993.

Eng. William F. *Trading Rules: Strategies for Success.* Chicago: Dearborn, 1990.

Friedfertig, Marc and West, George. *The Electronic Day Trader.* New York: McGraw Hill, 1998.

Gann, W.D. *How to Make Profits Trading in Commodities.* Pomeroy: Lambert-Gann, 1976.

Gold, LauraMaery and Post, Dan. *J.K. Lasser's Invest Online*. New York: Macmillan, 1999.

Houtkin, Harvey and Waldman, David. *Secret of the SOES Bandit*. New York: McGraw Hill, 1998.

Koppel, Robert. *Bulls, Bears and Millionaires: War Stories of the Trading Life*. Chicago: Dearborn, 1997.

Koppel, Robert. *The Intuitive Trader: Developing Your Inner Market Wisdom*. New York: John Wiley, 1996.

Koppel, Robert. *The Tao of Trading*. Chicago: Dearborn, 1997.

Koppel, Robert and Abell, Howard. *The Innergame of Trading: Modeling the Psychology of the Top Traders*. New York: McGraw Hill, 1993.

Koppel, Robert and Abell, Howard. *The Outer Game of Trading: Modeling the Trading Strategies of Today's Market Wizards*. New York: McGraw Hill, 1994.

Le Bon, Gustave. *The Crowd: A Study of the Popular Mind*, 2d ed. Atlanta: Cherokee, 1982.

Markman, Jon D. *Online Investing*. Redmond: Microsoft Press, 1999.

O'Neil, William. *How to Make Money in Stocks*. New York: McGraw-Hill, 1995.

Schwager, Jack D. *Market Wizards: Interviews with Top Traders*. New York: New York Institute of Finance, 1989.

Schwager, Jack D. *The New Market Wizards: Conversations with America's Top Traders*. New York: Harper Business, 1992.

Schwartz, Martin. *Pit Bull: Lessons from Wall Street's Champion Trader*. New York: Harper Business, 1998.

Sperandeo, Victor with Brown T. Sullivan. *Trader Vic—Methods of a Wall Street Master*. New York: John Wiley & Sons, 1991.

Glossary

Advance/decline line A measure of market movements composed of the cumulative total of differences between advancing issues (stocks whose prices are up on the day) and declining issues (stocks whose prices are down on the day) of securities prices.

American style options Options that may be exercised any time prior to the expiration date.

Ask The lowest currently stated acceptable price for a specific stock or commodity on the floor of an exchange. Also called the offer.

Assignment The process by which the seller of an option is notified of the buyer's intention to exercise.

At-the-money An option in which the price of the underlying instrument is exactly the same as the strike price of the option.

Bear Anyone who takes a pessimistic view of the forthcoming long-term trend in a market: that is, one who thinks that a market is or soon will be in a long-term downtrend.

Bear market A long-term downtrend (a downtrend lasting months to years) in any market, especially in the stock market, characterized by lower intermediate lows interrupted by lower intermediate highs.

Bear spread Any spread in which a fall in the price of the underlying security will theoretically increase the value of the spread.

Bid An indication by an investor, trader, or dealer of the willingness to buy a security or a commodity at a certain price. Also, the highest current such indication for a specific stock or commodity at any point in time.

Bid and ask The current quote or quotation of any market for a specific stock or commodity.

Block A large amount of specific stock, generally 10,000 shares or more.

Blue chip The common stock of an established industry leader whose products or services are widely known and which has a solid record of performance in both good and bad economic environments.

Bottom The lowest price within a market movement that occurs before the trend changes and starts moving up.

Book value A measure of the net worth of a share of common stock.

Break A downward price movement that goes below previous important lows and continues downward.

Breakout An upward price movement that goes above previous important highs and continues upward.

Bull Anyone who takes an optimistic view of the forthcoming long-term trend in a market: that is, one who thinks that a market is or soon will be in a long-term uptrend.

Bull market A long-term price movement in any market characterized by a series of higher intermediate highs interrupted by higher consecutive intermediate lows.

Bull spread Any spread in which a rise in the price of the underlying security will theoretically increase the value of the spread.

Butterfly spread An option position involving the simultaneous buying of an at-the-money option, selling two out-of-the-money options, and buying one out-of-the-money option.

Call option A short-term or medium-term contract that allows the purchaser the right, but not the obligation, to go long the underlying investment at the strike price on or before the option expiration date. An option seller receives the premium and assumes the obligation to go long or short the underlying investment at the strike price if the option is exercised.

Commission The fee charged to a client by a registered broker for the execution of an order to buy or sell a stock, bond, commodity, option, etc.

Correction An intermediate market price movement that moves contrary to the long-term trend.

Covered position A combination of an underlying investment and an options transaction that is theoretically less risky than either individual part of the transaction.

Delta The sensitivity (rate of change) of an option's theoretical value (assessed value) to changes in the price of the underlying instrument. Expressed as a percentage, it represents an equivalent amount of the underlying at a given moment in time. Calls have positive deltas; puts have negative deltas.

Dow Jones Industrial Average (DJIA) The most widely used indicator of market activity, composed of an average of 30 large issues within the industrial sector of the economy.

Dow Jones Transportation Average (TRAN) The most widely reported indicator of stock activity in the transportation sector of the economy, composed of an average of 20 large issues.

Dow Jones Utility Average (UTIL) The most widely reported indicator of stock activity in the utility sector, composed of 15 gas, electric, and power company issues.

Earnings The net income available for common stock, divided by the number of shares outstanding, reported quarterly by most companies. (Also earnings-per-share.)

European-style options Options that may be exercised on the expiration date only.

Exercise The process by which the buyer of an option notifies the seller of his or her intention to take delivery of the underlying in the case of a call, or make delivery, in the case of a put, at the specified exercise price.

Exercise price The price at which the underlying will be delivered in the event the option is exercised.

Expiration The date an option contract becomes worthless. All buyers of options must indicate their desire to exercise by this date.

Fade Doing the opposite of the immediate market movement.

Flat Having no position.

Floor trader A member of an exchange who enters transactions for his or her own account from the floor of the exchange: synonymous with local.

Glamour stock A favored, highly traded stock, usually of an established company that has performed well and paid dividends in good times and bad.

Growth stock A relatively speculative stock, usually one of a relatively new company that is expected to grow at a fast rate.

High The highest price a security or commodity reaches within a specified time period.

Index A composite of stocks (e.g., Dow Jones, S&P, and Nasdaq).

Index futures Futures contracts traded on the basis of an underlying cash index or average.

In the money (ITM) A call is in the money if its strike is lower than the market price of the underlying. A put is in the money if its strike price is higher than the market price of the underlying.

Intrinsic value (also called parity) The amount by which an option is in the money. Out of the money (OTM) options have no intrinsic value.

Long Position resulting from the purchase of a contract or instrument.

Long-term trend Price movements tending to be generally up or generally down lasting over a period of months to years.

Low The lowest price of a security or commodity reached during a specific time period.

Margin The amount of equity (cash) as a percentage of market value of the underlying market interest held in a margin account.

Neutral spread A position that has virtually no exposure to the conditions of a market. Also known as flat or square.

Offer An indication by a trader or investor of the willingness to sell a security or commodity: or, in a quote, the current lowest price anyone is willing to sell a security or commodity.

Out of the money (OTM) An option which has no intrinsic value. A call is out of the money if its strike price is higher than the current market price of the underlying. A put is out of the money if its strike price is lower than the current price of the underlying.

Over the counter (OTC) market A market of stocks traded that are not listed on the major exchanges.

Put Option An option contract that gives the buyer the right but not the obligation to sell the underlying investment at a specific price on or before a specific date.

Quote The current bid and offer for a security on the floor of the exchange on which it is traded.

Ratio writing A market position using more than one option to hedge an investment position.

Resistance Any price level that is deemed as a significant high in trading by the market and offers a place to sell the market.

S&P futures A futures index traded based on the S&P 500 Cash Index.

Short A position resulting from the sale of a contract or instrument. To sell a contract without, or prior to, buying it.

Stop order An order given to a broker that becomes a market order when the market price of the underlying instrument reaches or exceeds the specific price stated in the stop order.

Spread A position that is both long and short in the same investment with different expiration dates, or long or short different but similar investments.

Straddle An options position consisting of a call and put in the same investment, same expiration, and same strike price.

Strangle A position in which one buys (or sells) both an out of money put and an out of money call.

Support Any price level deemed as a significant low in trading by the market, which offers a place to buy the market.

Synthetic Two or more trading vehicles combined to emulate another, or spread. Because the package involves different components, price is also different although the risk usually is the same.

Technical analysis A method of market forecasting that relies exclusively on the study of past price and volume behavior to predict future price movements.

Underlying The instrument (stock, future, or cash index) to be delivered when an option is exercised. The amount of underlying for each option contract depends on the security traded. For example, in stock options, each contract represents 100 shares of the underlying stock.

Volatility The degree to which the price of an underlying tends to change over time. This variable, which the market implies to the underlying, may result from pricing an option through a model.

Volume The number of shares of stocks that change ownership in a given time period.

Index

A

Abell, Howard, 11–12, 30, 64
Accounts receivable turnover, 28
Accumulation phase, 133–34
Acid-test ratio, 28
Action plan, 45
Activity measurements, 28
ADX, 187
Agatstein, Gene, 41, 80
American Stock Exchange, 9
Ameritrade, 9
Anger, 73
Anxiety, 81–90
    sources of, 81, 82
    strategies for controlling, 83–87
    strengths and weaknesses,
        identifying, 88–90
Apple Computer, 175
Arbor, Pat, 13
Ascending triangle, 139
Attitude(s), 4, 12–17, 88. *See also*
    Imagery, positive; State of mind
Auditory imagery, 106
Automated electronic execution
    system, 10
Averaging a loss, 25

B

Bar patterns, one- or two-day, 179–84
Baruch, Bernard, 5, 76–77
Behavior, constructing new patterns
    of, 51–52
Beliefs, 13–14, 61–62, 88
    positive, and state of mind, 106–7
Berra, Yogi, 78
Bias, of markets, 113
Bollinger Bands, 187

Book of the Five Rings, The, 16
Book value per share, 27
Bottom picking, 25
Bottoms, 135
Bottom test, 192
Breakaway gap, 142
Breakout, 79, 190, 193
Breakout above accumulation, 134–35
Breakout trades, 151–53
Buffett, Warren, 26
Bull market, 20–21
Busch, Arlene, 52

C

CANSLIM, 21
Channel breakout, 117–18
Channel support and resistance, 128–30
Charles Schwab, 6
Chart analysis, 125–31
    continuation patterns, 136–39, 140
    gaps, 139–44, 145
    retracements, 130–31
    reversal patterns, 135–36, 137
    support and resistance, 128–30
Chatrooms, 3
Churchill, Winston, 86
Climaxes, buying and selling, 29
Commissions, 25
Commitment, 48–50
Common gap, 140, 141
Competing, 205–17
    mental toughness, maintaining,
        205–6
    state of mind, 207–14
Computer-generated numbers, 184–87
Computer networking stocks, 47
Conditioning, 52–53

Confidence, 61, 67–80, 98, 212
  identifying market signal, 77
  learning to take a loss, 73–76
  trading syntax, 76–77
Confusion, 72–73
Consistency, 30, 87, 212
Constricted-range day, 173, 184, 185, 190–94
Continuation patterns, 136–39, 140
Control, fear of loss of, 82
Conviction, 50–51
Courage, 11
Crabel, Tony, 89
Csikszentmihalyi, Mihaly, 97
Current ratio, 28

D

Daily patterns, 173–74
Davis, Rod, 4
Day trader, 29–30
Debt to asset ratio, 28
Debt to equity ratio, 28
Denial, 72
Descending triangle, 139
Digital Day Trading, 64
Discipline, 4, 30, 31, 35, 52, 60, 98, 212
Discount brokerage, 10
Distribution phase, 135
Diversification, 19
Dividend payout, 27
Double bottom with ID, 191–92, 194
Double bottom with next-day buy, 193, 195
Double top next-day sell, 194, 196
Dow Jones Industrial Average, 20–21, 22
Downside breakout, 128

E

Earnings growth, 21
Earnings per share, 27

ECNs, 10
Economic conditions, 21
Edge, 59–65, 85
Education, 215
Ego, 208
Electronic communication networks (ECNs), 10
Electronic Trading of Options, The, 30
Elliot Wave, 170
Emerson, Ralph Waldo, 209
Energizing thoughts, 99
Energy, lack of, 58
E*Trade, 68
Euphoric trading, 79
Exhaustion gap, 143, 145
Expectations, for self, 209–10
Expertise, 60
Expirations, 30
External dimension strategies, 87–88

F

Failure, fear of, 82
Fan pattern, 130
Fast market conditions, 166
Fast moving average, 118, 119
Fear, 14–15, 20, 68, 70, 82
Fibonacci .682, 170, 175, 178
Fixed commissions, 10
Flag patterns, 172
Flags, 137–38, 139
Flexibility, 11
Flow, 97
Flow: The Psychology of Optimal Experience, 97
Focus, 30, 37, 57–58, 62–63, 84, 88, 92–93
Forrester Research, 6

G

Gallwey, Timothy, 45
Gann Fan lines, 171
Gaps, 139–44, 145

Gindof, Bryan, 46–48
Goals, 31, 43–65, 60, 84, 88, 211
    action plan, developing, 45
    adjusting, 45
    commitment and, 48–50
    conditioning and, 52–53
    constructing new behavior
        patterns and, 51–52
    conviction and, 50–51
    criteria for, 54–56
    getting the edge, 59–65
    importance of, 54
    monthly goal chart, 56
    overcoming impediments, 56–58
    specific outcomes and, 44
    traders and, 45–48
Goodspeed, Bennett W., 35
Government policies, 21
Greed, 20
Greenberg, Joel, 40
Grossman, Tom, 49–50, 69

H–I

How to Make Money in Stocks, 21
Humor, 209
Huxley, Thomas, 207
Imagery, positive, 103–9
    implementing visualizations/
        beliefs, 107–8
    optimizing, 108–9
    projection, 104–5
    winning state of mind, 105
Inaction, 72
Independence, 212
Inflation, expectations of, 21
Information, stock selection and, 149
Inner Game of Tennis, The, 45
Innergame of Trading, The, 8, 14
Inner/outer games, 87–88
Inside day, 173, 183–84
Interest rates, 21
Internal dimension strategies, 87–88
Internet investing, 6, 215

Intuition, 64, 211
Intuitive Trader, 92
Inventory turnover ratio, 28
Investing mistakes, 21, 25
Investors, characteristics of successful,
    11–16. *See also* Success
Island reversal, 143, 146

J–K

James, Henry, 4
Jensen, Jeff, 213
Judgment, 11
Kamikaze trading, 79
Key reversal, 135
Kinesthetic imagery, 106
King, Winston L., 16

L

Lefevre, Edwin, 71
Leonard, George, 31–32
Leventhal, Linda, 92–93
Leverage measurements, 28
Levitt, Arthur, 215
Liquidity, 28, 148
Loehr, James E., 32, 98, 99, 205
Long-term investor, 27–28
Long-term trader, 29
Loss, 25, 71, 78, 84, 85, 190, 212
    dealing with, 71–73
    taking, 68, 73–76

M

McAuliffe, Tim, 68
McKinsey & Co., 6
MACD, 187
Main phase, 134–35
Management, 21
Market entry point, 160
Market exit point, 161–62
Market makers, 29

Market phases, trends and, 133–35
    accumulation phase, 133–34
    distribution phase, 135
    main phase, 134–35
Market psychology, sideways trends
    and, 128–30
Market retracements, 170–71
Market signal, identifying, 77
Market strategy (strategies), 25–26,
    37, 83–87
    internal and external, 87–88
    and tactics compared, 81
Market Wizards, 17
Mastery, 31–32
Measuring gap, 143, 144
Melamed, Leo, 8, 13, 40
Mencken, H.L., 43
Mendoza, Mariano, 214
Mental Game, The, 32, 99
Mesch, Robin, 51–52
Mistakes, 21, 25
Money management, 80, 119–23, 211
    swing trader and, 162–64
Money Talks, 5
Morgan, J.P., 83
Motivation, 35–41, 54, 60, 88
    common reasons for online
        trading, 37
    lessons of top traders, 39–41
    trading strategy and, 83
Moving average, 116–17, 127–28,
    196–98
    see also Fast moving average
    market retracements to, 171
Mulmat, Peter, 64
Musashi, Miyamoto, 16
Mutual funds, 19–20

N

Nasdaq, 10, 21, 24
National Association of Securities
    Dealers, 10
New high breakout, 190, 193
New Market Wizards, The, 211

New York Stock Exchange, 9
Noe, John R., 14
Noise, 166
Nordstrom Corporation, 83

O

O'Neil, William J., 21
Online trading, 10, 39, 147–57
    patterns, 150–57
    statistics, 6
    stock selection criteria, 148–50
    trading evolution, 9–10
    traders, categories of, 27–32
        day trader, 29–30
        long-term investor, 27–28
        long-term trader, 29
        options trader, 30–32
        swing trader, 29
Opportunities, identifying, 87
Options trader, 30–32
Oscillator, 184, 186, 187
Outcome goal, 54. *See also* Goals
Outside day, 173, 183
Over-the-counter market (OTC), 9

P

Parker, Dorothy, 12
Patience, 31, 60, 86, 165, 212
Pattern recognition, 179
*Peak Performing Principles for High
    Achievers*, 14
Performance goal, 54. *See also* Goals
Performance-enhancing imagery, 106
Persistence, 32
Personality,
    investment method and, 211
    market strategy and, 85
Pitfalls, 25
Pivot numbers, 184–86
Pliability, 11
Plummer, Tony, 71
Positive imagery, 103–9

Positive state of mind, 61
Predetermined buy/sell areas, 165
Price-earnings ratio, 27
Price level, stock selection and,
   149–50
Price retracements, 29
Price to book ratio, 27
Product development, 21
Productivity, 21
Profit, 78
Profitability measurements, 27
Profit margin, 27
Profit-orientation, 86
Prudence, 11
Psychological barriers, overcoming,
   56–69, 78–80, 139, 144–46
      controlling anxiety, 81–90
      poor money management and,
         120
Psychological characteristics, of
   winning state of mind, 105
Psychological skills, 36, 76–77
      buying a breaking market and,
         125
      communicating with self, 208–9
      creating internal environment for
         success, 207–8
      getting the "edge," 59–65
Psychology of Technical Analysis, The,
   71

R

Raschke, Linda Bradford, 183
Rectangles, 137–38, 139
Reenergizing, 109
Reentry, based on trendline, 127
Reminiscences of a Stock Operator, 71
Research, 25, 26
Resourcefulness, 94–95
Responsibility, 83, 211–14
Retracements, 118, 121, 130–31,
   153–54, 155
Return on equity, 20, 27
Returns, 30

Reversal patterns, 135–36, 137
Reynolds, Angelo, 50
"Riding the Mo in the Lime Green
   Glow," 76
Risk, 84, 85, 211
      control, 31, 60
      parameters, 29
      /reward characteristics, 30
Robbins, Anthony, 14, 87
Rockne, Knute, 207
RSI, 187
Rubinstein, Arthur, 209–10
Rumors, 3

S

Saliba, Tony, 13
Samurai analogy, 93
Sandner, Jack, 15–16, 62–64, 69
Scalping, 29, 150
Schwager, Jack, 17, 211
Securities and Exchange Commission
   (SEC), 10
Securities Industry Association, 215
Securities ratios, 27
Segal, George, 78
SelectNet System, 10
Self-control, 98
Self-discipline, 4, 98
Self-limiting beliefs, 57
Self-motivation, 36–37
Self-realization, 98
Self-reliance, 11
Self-talk, 108
Setup(s), 165, 166–74
      chart, 168–74
      computer, 167, 169
      market, 167, 168
Seykota, Ed, 17
Shanks, Tom, 46
Short-term traders, marketing strategy,
   25–26
Sideways trend, 128, 185
Siegel, Joseph, 41
Silverman, Jeffery, 13, 72–73

Sliter, Donald, 92
Small Order Execution System
    (SOES), 10
Snap back, 198–99
Spitzer, Eliot, 215
Sponsorship, stock selection and, 149
Standard of excellence, 207, 211
Standard & Poor's 500 Stock Index,
    21, 23
State of mind, 60, 61, 80, 88, 91–101
    see also Imagery, positive
    competing and, 207–14
    creative thought and
        performance, 99–100
    energizing thoughts, 99
    flow, 97
    4-step program, 98
    keys to success and, 101
    trading strategy and, 95–96
Stein, Marshall, 50–51
Stocastics, 187
Stock selection criteria, 148–50
Stock trading patterns, 150–57
    breakout trades, 151–53
    retracement trades, 153–54, 155
    tests, 154–57
Strategies, 19, 59, 62
    see also Market strategy
        (strategies)
    basic trading, 26–27
    ill-defined personal, 58
    marketing, 25–26
    state of mind and, 95–96
Strengths, identifying, 88–90
Strike prices, 30
Success
    characteristics of, 11–16
    fear of, 82
    psychological barriers to, 78–80
    state of mind and, 101
    trading syntax and, 70, 76–77
Support and resistance, channel,
    128–30
Support and resistance, trendline, 130
Suretrade, 8–9
Suzuki, 93

Swing trader, 29
Swing trading, 150, 159–87
    creating road map for, 174–87
    bar patterns, 179
    computer-generated
        numbers, 184–87
    pattern recognition, 179,
        181–84
    swing location of market,
        178–79
    trend identification, 175–78
    market entry point, 160
    market exit point, 161–62
    money management, 162–64
    setups, 166–74
    trading method, 164–66
    trend identification, 159–60,
        175–78
Symmetrical triangle, 139

T

Tao Jones Averages, The, 35
Tao of Trading, 93
Tao Te Ching, 210
Taylor, George, 178
Taylor Trading Techniques, The, 178
Technical analysis, psychology of,
    113–23
    money management, 119–23
    trends, and efficient market
        theory, 114–19
Technical indicators, 29
Tests, 154–57, 190, 191, 192, 199
Three- to five-day swings, 168
Tinker, Grant, 207
Toppel, Edward, 96
Tops, 135, 137, 194–96
TORCH FIRE, 208–9
Total asset turnover, 28
Total return (mutual funds), 27
Total return (stock), 27
Trading evolution, 9–10
Trading goals. See Goals
Trading intuition, 64

Trading success, 189–201
 automatic action, 190
 feeling good about a trade, 190
 identifying opportunity, 190
Trading systems, 113–14
 entry/exit of market positions,
  118, 119, 120, 121
 money management, 119–23
 trend identification, 114–18
Trend(s)
 chart analysis and, 125–31
 continuation patterns, 136–39,
  140
 defined, 113
 establishing uptrends/
  downtrends, 115
 gaps, 139–44, 145
 identification, 114–18, 159–60,
  175–77
 long-term market, 20–21
 market position entry/exit and,
  118–19
 moving averages and, 116
 phases of, 133–35
 reversal patterns, 135–36
 trendline pullbacks, 29
 trendlines, 198
Triangle patterns, 172, 179, 181
Triangles, 137–39
Two-day highs and lows, 173
Two-day test, 199–200

U

Undervalued stock, 28
Unlimited Power, 14
Unresourceful state, 57
Upside breakout, 128
Uptrend, 125–26

V–W

Visualization. *See* Imagery, positive
Volatility, 148
Watts, Dickson G., 11
Weaknesses, identifying, 88–90
*What You Need to Know before You
 Invest,* 4
Wide-range day, 173
Wooden, John, 98
Working capital, 28

Y–Z

Youngman, Henny, 78
Zen and the Japanese Culture, 93
Zen and the Markets, 96
*Zen and the Way of the Sword, Arming
 the Samurai Psyche,* 16
Ziglar, Zig, 15
"Zone," 92

About the Author

Robert Koppel is president of the Invest2Know.com, a financial education Web site. He is the author of *The Tao of Trading* (Dearborn, 1998), *Bulls, Bears and Millionaires* (Dearborn, 1997), and *The Intuitive Trader* (Wiley, 1996). He is coauthor of *The Innergame of Trading* (McGraw-Hill, 1993), *The Outer Game of Trading* (McGraw-Hill, 1994), and *The Market Savvy Investor* (Dearborn, 1999). He is a former long-term member of the Chicago Mercantile Exchange and senior editor for online trading at OnMoney.com. He holds advanced degrees in Philosophy and Group Behavior from Columbia University.

For more information about trader education, please contact:
Bob Koppel
Invest2Know.com
141 West Jackson Blvd.
Suite 1950
Chicago, IL 60604
800-726-3088
312-559-8898
email: bob@Invest2Know.com